CAREER
PSYCHOLOGY

CAREER PSYCHOLOGY

Practical Career Support From a
Recruiter and Counselor

Dan Joseph Cavicchio, LPC

quiet
mind

Quiet Mind Publishing, LLC
PO Box 2017
Boulder, CO 80306

Copyright © 2022 by Dan Joseph Cavicchio

Cavicchio, Dan Joseph
Career Psychology: Practical Career Support From a
  Recruiter and Counselor
ISBN: 9798833126769

All rights reserved. No part of this book may be republished, reproduced, stored in a retrieval or archival system, or transmitted in any form or by any means, electronic, mechanical, recording, or otherwise, without the prior written permission of the author.

The material in this book is provided solely for informational and educational purposes. It does not substitute for professional counseling or therapy. Information in this book does not represent clinical advice for treatment of psychological disorders.

Contact the author at https://www.FreeCareerBook.com.

My deep gratitude to my wife Carol, my friends Angela and Brad, and the many other people who assisted with this book.

Thank you also to my counseling and corporate clients who have allowed me to help with your career development and team building needs.

Contents

Introduction
9

Chapter One
A Bit About Me
11

Chapter Two
Exploring Career Paths: The Five Questions
21

Chapter Three
Exploring Career Paths: A Deeper Look
49

Chapter Four
The Job Search
69

Chapter Five
The Job Search: A Deeper Look
99

Chapter Six
Resumes, Cover Letters, and Applications
115

Chapter Seven
Resumes, Cover Letters, and Applications:
A Deeper Look
141

Chapter Eight
Interviews
155

Chapter Nine
Interviews: A Deeper Look
185

Chapter Ten
Self-Employment
199

Chapter Eleven
Self-Employment: A Deeper Look
223

Chapter Twelve
Increasing Your Happiness at Work
231

Chapter Thirteen
Increasing Your Happiness at Work:
A Deeper Look
257

Chapter Fourteen
Action Steps
271

INTRODUCTION

Let me begin this book by introducing myself.

For the past twenty years I have worked as an executive and technical recruiter, helping companies to find employees. I write job ads, reach out to candidates, negotiate salaries, and smooth out bumps in order to close employment deals.

That's my day job.

At night, I run a private practice as a licensed counselor and psychotherapist, specializing in career counseling and cognitive behavioral therapy. I help people explore career options, write resumes, start businesses, and deal with work-related stress, anxiety, and interpersonal conflicts.

My two worlds never cross. I never, for example, recruit a counseling client into a job I'm trying to fill. But I have worked on both sides of the employment table, and understand the different perspectives.

My goal in writing this book is to support you in your career journey. Maybe you are looking for your first job. Or perhaps you are seeking a more fulfilling type of work. You might be considering a switch to self-employment. In this book, I'll offer assistance for those situations and more.

The world of work can be challenging at times. I know the sense of pressure and isolation that many jobs involve. I know how unsettling it can be to leave a career path, and feel cast adrift. I know what it's like to set up a business, give it your all, and have it struggle to stay afloat.

I also know what it's like to find a career that simply feels right—a career that brings fulfillment while making a positive impact on the world. My aim is to help you find that.

In this book, I'll share both psychological tools and practical information to help navigate the work world. Whether you're at the beginning of your career, making a change of direction, or simply looking for next steps along an established path, I will try to offer assistance.

You're invited to bounce around in this book. If you would like help with job searching or resume writing, feel free to jump ahead to those chapters. If self-employment is of interest, you can begin by reading that part.

I've covered a variety of career-related subjects, and followed each with a series of questions and answers. However, you may not need assistance with all of these topics. Please flip through this book as you see fit.

One of the top "interview techniques" that I recommend to my clients is to draw on personal stories when building a relationship. Personal experiences are humanizing, and help to form connections.

In the spirit of that, let me begin this book by sharing a few brief stories about my own early work history.

CHAPTER ONE

A Bit About Me

When I was first learning to read, my favorite book was Richard Scarry's *What Do People Do All Day?* If you haven't read it as a child (or with your kids), it's a colorful look into the lives of workers.

I used to spend hours studying the pictures in that book: the farmer growing corn to sell to the store owner, the baker who would grind the corn and turn it into bread, the folks underground working on the pipes and electrical lines.

It was all utterly fascinating. I would wear out every copy of the book, eventually breaking the binding and forcing my parents to buy me another version. We probably went through a half-dozen copies by the time I was five years old.

I never felt attracted to any one profession in the book. I simply wanted to understand how it all worked. I had an insatiable desire to see the whole system.

One day I asked my parents: "Do you have to choose a single job? Or can you do more than one?" They assured me that there were no rules about things like that, and I was extremely relieved to hear it.

Years later, I have engaged in many types of work. I have counseled men coming out of prison. I have recruited CEOs. I have worked on road-paving crews, designed websites, coached entrepreneurs, written freelance articles, and done a number of other things.

Each of those experiences gave me some insights into the world of work, many of which I'll share in this book.

Let me begin with a story about my first job.

•

I grew up in a small town just north of New York City. As a kid, I spent my free time behind a computer playing games and dreaming of the day when I could upgrade my old machine to something more powerful.

Shortly after I turned fourteen, I walked into the local computer store and asked if I could get a job selling video games.

I remember two men looking at each other and chuckling.

"We have professional salespeople for that," they said.

"But I've played almost all the games you have here," I told them, pointing at the wall full of boxes. "I know them all."

"I'm sure you do," they said, "but we don't hire people your age for sales jobs."

"Maybe I can help your salespeople," I said. "I can tell them which of these games are the best."

One of them thought for a moment.

He said, "We might have a part-time job helping around the store. Not software sales, just basic stuff. Would you be interested in that?"

I figured that it was an opening, so I took him up on his offer. After securing a work permit, I started my first job.

It was ridiculously boring. I vacuumed the carpet, unloaded computers from the trucks, broke down cardboard boxes, and emptied the trash bins. That was it. Otherwise, all of us in the store waited around for customers or deliveries to roll in, and watched the clock to see how long we had before closing time arrived.

The pay was minimum-wage—just over $3/hour—and I knew nothing about tax withholding. When I received my first paycheck, I was stunned. That was it? All those bus trips to the store in the dark and cold, all that time taking out the garbage and waiting around with nothing else to do—all that for $45?

This wasn't fun, like work appeared in my childhood book. This was sort of depressing. After a few months (and another unsuccessful pitch or two to sell video games), I stopped asking to be put on the schedule. No one seemed to care that I wasn't in anymore.

But then, about six months later, I realized something.

I remembered that another young man who worked with me had purchased a computer "at cost." He had received a 50% discount on his purchase. That, apparently, was one of the perks of working at the store.

I ran the math and realized that I could work a few months, sell my old computer, and buy a powerful new model with my employee discount. Suddenly, the store seemed like a *very* interesting place to work.

So I called in, requested a shift, and showed back up at work. A few people were surprised to see me, but they shrugged and let me return to emptying the trash pails.

Things were different now, though. I had a deeper reason for being at the job. I saved up my money for several months, sold my old computer, and bought a glorious new machine to play the best games.

That experience showed me the value of purpose. During my first round at the store, I had no great reason to be at that minimum-wage job versus any other. But during round two, I had a mission—a vision. My experience of work was completely different because of that.

As a cognitive behavioral therapist, I frequently draw on this insight with clients. Our thoughts, including the *purpose* we associate with our work, influence our emotional experience of our careers.

I often ask my counseling clients questions like:

In addition to earning money, what is your reason for doing the type of work that you do?
What is your purpose in your current job?
What is your personal "mission" in your work life?

Most of my clients struggle to answer those questions. They say, "To be honest, Dan, I've never thought about things like that."

Through our conversations, we clarify their values. We choose a meaningful purpose for their activities. This often shifts the emotional landscape of their work lives considerably.

Some of my clients end up staying at their existing jobs, armed with a new mission that reorients their approach. Others have a clearer vision about new opportunities they want to seek, and why they want to seek them. This helps them forge a new career path.

I'll delve into this topic in greater detail later in this book, as I consider it to be important.

For now, let me share another story.

•

The next summer, at age fifteen, I was spending my time playing games on my new computer. I mowed lawns on occasion to make money, and was looking to earn a bit more.

One day, a man knocked on the door of our house.

"I'm with a road paving company," the man told my mother. "You'll need to keep your cars off the street tomorrow."

"You know, I have a son who is looking for work," my mother said to him. "Does your company need help?"

"Sure," he said, "We can always use some extra hands. If your son is interested, have him come down to our staging location."

When she told me about this development, I didn't know what to think.

Join a road crew? With those giant machines that I had seen around town? At age fifteen?

Nevertheless, I decided to check it out. I biked down to a site in the Bronx early the next morning and introduced myself to the foreman. He confirmed that they could use some help, and would be in our town through the end of the week.

I filled out some tax paperwork. We never discussed the pay rate, although I assumed it would be minimum wage like my computer store job.

For a week, I rode around with the staging crew. At the beginning of the day, we pried up manhole covers, layered them with plastic, and laid them back down. After the paving machines coated the street, we set up sawhorses and cones to block traffic.

I then sat next to the newly paved roads, and stopped anyone from driving on the wet asphalt.

Finally, at the end of the day, we cleared the plastic from the manhole covers, removed the sawhorses and cones, and packed everything back up in the truck.

That was it. I worked for a week doing that.

On the last day, I asked how I would get paid. The foreman said, "We'll mail you a check. However, I'm not sure how our accounting system is set up. It might turn out that you qualify for union wages."

To my great shock, I received a check for well over $1000. I had been paid an entire summer's worth of minimum-wage work in a week.

It was a stunning amount of money. But here's the interesting thing: That job was intolerable to me. I would have quit at the end of the week, even if I knew how much they were paying me.

And why? Because I had to spend hours by myself each day, in silence, sitting by the road with nothing but my thoughts to distract me. The experience was miserable.

Since then, I have learned—and taught my clients—a variety of mindfulness and centering practices. These days, I would find a day spent alone in silence to be delightful. But back then, it was the opposite.

My days with the road crew remind me of the story about a man seeking enlightenment.

The man hikes up to a monastery in the mountains. "I'm here to find inner peace," he says to the head monk.

The monk tells him, "OK, you're welcome to stay with us. But there are some jobs I'd like you to do. To begin, please move that pile of rocks to the other side of the monastery."

The man does as he's told. After a week, he has moved all the rocks.

"Now," says the monk, "move the rocks back."

"But I just spent a week moving them!" the man says.

"Yes," says the monk, "and you'll move the rocks back and forth and back again. When you've learned how to do the work in a state of peace, then you'll have what you came here for."

When I first heard that story, I thought it was silly. Spending days moving rocks back and forth? Why waste effort on such a pointless activity?

But now I appreciate the story. Our activities aren't pointless; they serve whatever goals we set for them. The man at the monastery moved rocks with the goal of attaining peace. I, sitting by the side of the road at fifteen, could have brought my own goals to my work each day.

My daily goal could have been to improve people's lives by being friendly and protecting their cars from being damaged. Or my goal could have been to learn something by reading as I sat by the side of the road.

There were limitless goals I could have brought to my work. Instead, my only goal was to make it to the end of the day as I generated one frustrated and bored thought after another. It was not a pleasant experience.

However, like the man moving rocks, I actually gave it another shot.

The following summer, I happened to see a road crew paving the streets in my town once again. I went down to the staging site and told them I had worked with a different crew the previous summer. I asked if they needed help.

The company hired me again, although this time they let me drive the big truck full of sawhorses and cones. Having just received my driver's license, that was a thrill.

I became buddies with the staging guys. They even took me with them on their beer-drinking rounds after work. The experience was a bit more enjoyable this second time. And like before, I received a big check of union wages at the end.

•

Let me share one last story before moving on to the heart of this book.

The following summer, at age seventeen, I was hired as an intern at an urban planning non-profit company in Manhattan. It was my first experience in a corporate environment. I sat in a big, shared cubicle with my boss, and worked on spreadsheets and other computer tasks.

The place was formal and cold. The only humor in the office was the stray joke about saying "good-bye" versus "good-night" at closing time. A cup of coffee with a New York bagel was the high point of the day.

However, my boss was a kind woman, and the mission of the company involved things like environmental preservation—so I made the best of it, despite not liking the frosty vibe. I was relieved when my time there was over. I figured that perhaps urban planning just wasn't for me.

The next summer, I decided to give corporate life one more shot. I applied for various business internships, and landed a spot with a small New York company run by an alumnus of my college.

I vividly remember my on-campus interview with the CEO.

"You're so lucky to be here in school," he said to me.

We were sitting on a patio overlooking the main college green. It was a beautiful spring day. People were throwing frisbees and reading books under the trees.

"It's great," I said. "But I'm eager to get out into the real world. How is it there?"

"It sucks," he said. "The real world sucks."

And so it did!

At least, at that company of his.

His company manufactured generic brands of soaps and detergents out of a factory in New Jersey. It was not glamorous work. I spent the summer sitting alone at a makeshift desk in a hallway, uncomfortable in my suit and tie, trying to invent projects to work on while everyone ignored me.

I had never understood the term "soulless" until that summer. But wow—this was that. Isolating. Disconnected. Empty. If ever I could pop back in time and be my own therapist for a spell, this would be one of the top times to use the ability.

The one soulful thing I did that summer was to befriend a homeless man who sat on the street at 5th Avenue and 56th Street in Manhattan. I had some heartfelt conversations with him every day at lunch.

He was struggling; there was nothing easy about his life. But he was remarkably real and honest. It was the opposite of the empty, disconnected experience that I faced the rest of the time. My interaction with him was a lifeline, and to this day I am grateful to him for keeping me from slipping into a darker place.

When I returned to college in the fall, I began a reconsideration of my whole career path. I abandoned my interest in Wall Street and corporate finance and all the other things I had considered before.

ABOUT ME

I cleared the slate at that point in my life, and began a new journey through the world of work. In the rest of this book, I'll discuss some of what I learned in that process.

CHAPTER TWO

Exploring Career Paths: The Five Questions

When career counseling clients come to me, most of them are looking for a path—a professional track to follow, a career identity to call their own. Many of them know what they *don't* want to do. Now they are seeking a new direction.

I often begin by saying, "Please don't feel pressure to find one single path. You'll probably walk down many roads in your career. Those roads may branch in unexpected ways."

To illustrate how multifaceted career paths can be, I often share a few anecdotes about the different types of work I've done. Or I tell them about the career paths of other people in my life.

My mother, for example, earned a master's degree in teaching. She began her career by opening a house painting business. Then she sold children's books to libraries. On the weekends she officiated at weddings. In her retirement, she became a bed and breakfast host. These days she leads book study groups and creates inspirational TikTok videos.

My father wrote one of the world's first PhD dissertations on artificial intelligence back when computer data was stored on stacks of punch cards. Instead of going into computer science, he became a management consultant. After that, he and a partner took over a failing electronics factory and turned it around. They also purchased a scientific instruments company which he continues to run in his 70s.

My mother never became a classroom teacher, despite her degree. My father never went into computer science. Their paths unfolded in unpredictable and unique ways.

So it is with many of us. I have a friend who switched from being a lawyer to working as a musical performer at children's parties and schools. Two other friends did the opposite: They were school teachers before going into the law.

My dental hygienist was a server at a sushi restaurant before moving into dentistry. She married the sushi chef, who became a district attorney. My neighbor was an adventure tour guide who became a fireman, and then went into sales. Another friend worked as a massage therapist, a caregiver for a disabled adult, an appraiser, and a real estate developer.

There once was a time when people did one thing for the whole of their careers. But that time has largely passed. The world of work is now like an ocean with many currents. In order to navigate it, adaptability is key.

"But I have no idea where to begin!" some of my clients say.

I understand how overwhelming the nearly-endless career options can appear. Therefore, one of the first steps in career development is identifying a few steps to take down a path. As you walk forward, your own unique journey will unfold.

Let me share a note before continuing. Most career books focus on exploring different types of careers. I am going to do that as well, but *only* for this chapter and the one that follows. The rest of this book will offer practical steps and tools to move your work life forward.

I find that for most people, careers evolve through action. Careers do not pop into place through reading or analysis. Most people do not take a career assessment or read a book and say, "OK. Now I know what I'm going to spend my life doing!"

Instead, most people try a job (or many), switch career paths (usually more than once), meet people in other fields, volunteer, explore, observe, experiment, and see what unfolds.

Career development is a highly action-based process. There is no script for what is to come. The bulk of this book is designed to help you take active steps through the world of work, as you follow an inner sense of what's right for you. Your path will emerge as you walk forward.

Having said that, choosing an immediate career path to explore—even if it turns out to be a bridge to another path, and another—is an essential step in the process.

In this chapter I'll share a five-question career exploration framework that I use in my counseling practice.

Trait Factor Matching

Let me begin with a bit of career counseling history.

Back in the 1800s, there was a man named Frank Parsons. Frank had an interesting career path himself: He was a railroad worker, then a teacher, a lawyer, a textbook writer, and eventually the father of career counseling.

Frank developed something that we call *trait-factor matching*, and it has dominated career counseling approaches for over a hundred years. Here's the gist of the approach:

In the trait-factor matching process, you have two sets of information.

In Column A, you have a list of a person's skills and interests.

In Column B, you have a list of careers that fit those skills and interests.

You try to "match" Column A with Column B, in a logical way. Skills and interests here, careers that fit over there. It's very cut and dried (and computer-based, these days). You can see how attractive this is in our high-efficiency world.

Let's take someone named Mr. Smith as an example.

Mr. Smith likes to work with his hands. He hates being in an office. He has good dexterity. He doesn't like "people politics." He is physically strong.

CAREER PSYCHOLOGY

Now that we have Mr. Smith's information in Column A, let's look at the list of careers in Column B, and...what does the computer say...ah, yes. Here is his list of matches.

Mr. Smith's "traits" are a fit for a plumber, an electrician, a car mechanic, or an assembler in a factory. There are four matches for him to think about.

Mr. Smith	**Possible Careers**
Likes working with hands	√ Plumber
No office environment	√ Electrician
Has good dexterity	√ Car Mechanic
No people politics	√ Factory Assembler
Physically strong	Political Analyst
	Computer Engineer
	Accountant
	Sales Manager
	Musician

The process seems so simple and clear. But needless to say, modern life is very rarely clean-cut like that. Perhaps it was in the 1800s when the world of work was far less complex. Not anymore.

Most plumbers don't simply bang on pipes these days. Instead, they spend hours explaining complex concepts to clients, balancing aesthetic needs with technical ones, and training apprentices. They are creative problem-solvers, educators, and salespeople.

I've recruited factory assemblers who work in teams with extremely complex technology, interfacing with other divisions in the company. They use microscopes to align components, make calculations in spreadsheets, and help to create reports. Their teamwork skills are crucial.

My car mechanic spends a good part of his day dealing with frustrated or worried customers, and he's a master at soothing and de-escalation. The electricians I've come across range from high-voltage line workers to commercial installers to handymen, each requiring a plethora of related skills.

Will plumbing, assembly work, mechanical, or electrical work be a good fit for Mr. Smith? And if so, what type?

Who knows!

Mr. Smith will need to *actively explore* what's out there, trying out various roles and seeing what feels like a fit to him. No computer-based assessment will do that for him. And his career path will continually evolve as the world does, even if his core interests and skills remain somewhat stable.

With all respect to Frank Parsons, selecting a career path is rarely as simply as matching "traits" with careers that value those traits. And yet, much of career counseling these days involves this type of matching based an approach from over a hundred years ago.

I share this because I am going to take a different approach in this book. If the trait-factor matching approach appeals to you, I highly recommend a few sessions with a career counselor. Most counselors have access to various computer-based matching systems.

I myself use those tools at times. They can certainly be helpful, especially for recent graduates. However, in this book I will be taking a more creative, exploratory approach.

Focused Exploration

Let's begin the exploration of your work by talking about...a *vacation* from work.

Imagine that you just won a vacation to anywhere in the world. You can go anywhere you wish, all expenses paid. You can visit Africa, Asia, Europe, North America, South America—even

Antarctica. The world is your playground. It can be fun to consider the possibilities,

Where should you go?

You might begin your planning process by asking yourself a "focusing" question.

For example: Would you like to visit a big city? Or would you prefer to be in a more natural setting? Which of those two feels more interesting to you?

That's a very path-focusing question. Perhaps both environments have an appeal. For now, though—just for this one trip—you'll need to focus on one of those adventure types.

City or nature? Which of those places do you feel a pull?

A city setting like Tokyo, Paris, or Sydney? Or a natural site like the beaches of Hawaii, the snowy Alps, or the deserts of the Sahara?

You can go to the other type of environment on a future trip. This isn't the only vacation you'll take. But just for this one trip, which of those feels more interesting to you—city or nature?

Nature, you decide. At least for this trip.

Then another focusing question: Warm or cold? Something tropical and soothing, or something brisk and crisp? Where do you feel a pull?

Warm, you decide.

OK, warm it is. Now, would you like a warm place by the ocean? Or a rainforest? Or a desert retreat? Or a tropical cruise? What intrigues you? Where do you feel drawn?

Rainforest. That sounds fascinating.

And there we have it: By answering a few focusing questions, and following the "pull" that arose at each step, you were drawn to a destination.

You'll likely end up going to South America or Africa on your warm, nature-filled, rainforest vacation. We've defined a focused target for you to explore further.

That, in essence, is the type of approach I use in career counseling. To find your vacation spot, we didn't plug a bunch of data into a computer-based system to see what it spit out.

Instead, we asked some focusing questions and allowed your interests to guide you at each step. We still ended up with a destination, just as the trait-factor system does. But we followed your inner sense through the process, and didn't rely on algorithms.

Your exploration of careers can take the same approach. You can ask yourself a focusing question, notice where you feel pulled, and then move on to another focusing question. Your sense of what interests you will guide you further.

"Dan," some people say to me, "you don't like analytical approaches, do you?"

Actually, I'm quite analytical for a counselor. Plus I'm still a computer guy after all these years. But I am a firm, devoted believer that *your inner sense of what is right for you* is the most important compass to follow.

We actually took a very structured, precise approach in the vacation-choosing process: We asked one specific focusing question after another. But we didn't let outside data or computer systems guide your decision.

Instead, we trusted your inner compass—your inner sense of what appeals to you. We blended structure with intuition.

Clarifying the Compass

I've had some clients who listen to this and say, "Dan, I never have a good 'sense' of things. I find it almost impossible to choose a vacation place—much less a career path. Perhaps my inner compass is broken."

I tell them, "I don't believe your inner compass is broken. There is probably just some interference in the way."

To demonstrate the inner compass pull, I sometimes resort to humorous extremes. For example, I might say:

"I bet I can guess where you *don't* want to go on your next vacation."

"Yeah? Where is that?"

"Well, you said you're a big New York Yankees fan. I bet you wouldn't want to spend your vacation visiting Fenway Park in Boston. Cheer for the Red Sox and maybe get an autograph. Then you could head down to Shea Stadium to watch the Mets."

I get a look of horror from my client. "Oh, no! That sounds like the worst vacation ever! Anything but that."

"OK," I say, "it sounds like your compass is working just fine on that one. It's pointing you in the *opposite* direction of that. Let's now see what it is pointing you toward."

And then we return to our questions and exploration.

If you feel that it's difficult to get a sense of what interests or pulls you, feel free to read the Q&A chapter that follows this one. In that section, I'll share some "inner compass clarifying" techniques that I use with clients, including a hot-or-cold approach.

For now, though, let me run through five questions that I often ask my clients who are exploring new career paths. These questions are just a beginning, but I find that they can be very helpful in pointing toward next steps.

As you read through this, I invite you to consider how you might personally respond to each of these questions.

First Question

Every session I do with a client is unique. I try to follow my own inner sense about how to proceed, and there is no strict formula for what I am about to share.

Having said that, I often begin the career exploration process with the following basic questions. They help me to get a read on my client's interests, values, and orientations.

The first question I often ask people who are exploring career paths is this:

"Are you interested in working for an established organization, or would you prefer to be self-employed?"

Just like our city and nature vacation decision, this is a path focusing question.

As many as a third of all workers in the United States are at least partially self-employed. The other two-thirds work exclusively for an established company. So this question is important.

Many people jump at the self-employment option when I ask. At least, they do until I describe some of the elements that are very common in self-employment: a frequent emphasis on sales and business development, the need to handle a wide variety of roles, cash flow challenges.

I "pressure test" the answer when someone says that they want to be self-employed. I ask how comfortable the person will be with ebb-and-flow income cycles. I check to see if they feel capable doing their own accounting, taxes, and legal filings—or finding and paying a skilled accountant or lawyer. Above all, I ask if they are prepared to be in sales mode frequently, especially in the early stages of their business.

It usually becomes clear whether a person is truly feeling pulled toward the self-employment path. Those clients might say, "Dan, that sounds like a blast. I'm up for all the bumps and ups and downs. I love the idea of doing it all. I can't wait."

Or they might say, "Self-employment sounds scary, but it makes me feel alive. I want to at least give it a shot. I'd regret not trying. It's always something I wanted to do."

Other people quickly lose enthusiasm. They say, "Well, I figured I'd hire other people to do sales and all that." And they might—but likely, not at first.

At first, entrepreneurs usually need to do it all: sales and marketing, production, facilities management. For some people, self-employment begins to feel far less attractive as they consider managing all those various roles.

Let me ask you: Are you interested in working for an established company at this point in your career?

Working for a company, you will (hopefully) have a steady paycheck. Perhaps benefits, including paid vacation time. You'll have a team to work with, even if the team is tiny. You won't be asked to do everything. You'll have a supervisor to guide you, coworkers to chat with, and the company will not rest entirely on your shoulders.

Or does self-employment feel like a pull?

If so, can you create a daily schedule and structure for yourself, and stay on track even if no one is helping you? Are you comfortable living frugally if payments for your work are delayed or there is a seasonal lull? Are you excited about the hustle and hunt for customers, at least while you get started? Do you relish the chance to play multiple roles every day?

If your answer to these questions is yes, then self-employment may be for you.

There is a third option as well, although it's less common: a partnership. Do you have a friend or group of friends who might like to start a business with you? If so, do you share similar values, expectations, and goals? Will you and your partner(s) be able to split day-to-day responsibilities? Will you be able to resolve conflicts?

Try to get a sense of these paths as you consider the options. Does employment with an established company feel right? Or do you feel pulled toward self-employment? Or perhaps a partnership?

As you consider these, remember that we're focusing *only* on your immediate steps. No matter which path you choose, you can choose a different one in a month or a year. The road can always fork, branch, and turn. But just for now, at this point in your life, does one of these paths beckon to you?

If you're interested in self-employment and freelance paths, you're welcome to bounce ahead to chapter ten in this book. In my counseling practice, I frequently work with entrepreneurs, and I am delighted to support you. My self-employment chapter will probably be most relevant for your interests.

If you prefer to work with an established company, the next series of chapters are for you. You're in good company. The majority of people work for organizations rather than for themselves.

And of course, you can do both. I personally have spent most of my life employed part-time with a company (sometimes as a long-term contractor) and simultaneously running my own counseling, recruiting, and other businesses. You can aim for a blend if that feels ideal to you. In these days of the "side hustle," this combo approach is quite common.

> Questions if you're considering self-employment:
>
> Are you comfortable with the prospect of being in "sales" mode much of the time?
>
> Are you OK with your income ebbing and flowing, rather than being steady?
>
> Are you excited to "wear many hats" and engage in a variety of roles – everything from marketing to IT to accounting?
>
> Do you feel confident that you can set your own schedule day-to-day, and maintain your focus without outside support?
>
> If so, self-employment might be a good fit for you.

The next few questions are geared toward people seeking employment with established companies and organizations. Again, if self-employment is appealing to you, feel free to move right ahead to chapter ten.

Second Question: The Continuum

I usually draw a diagram for the next question. The diagram looks like this (though far messier on my white board):

For-Profit Companies	Middle-Way Organizations	Non-Profit Organizations

I show this to my clients, and ask them:

**"Do you feel attracted to the for-profit world?
Or the non-profit world?
Or perhaps something in the middle, like a school, a hospital, or a government group?"**

I call those last few "middle way organizations," because while some of them might technically be incorporated as for-profit and some as non-profit, they rest somewhere in the center of this diagram.

People who work in middle-way organizations like schools, hospitals, and government groups are in a unique place. They are not primarily focused on turning a profit. They're also not in the realm of the typical non-profit agency, with its emphasis on fundraising and low/no-fee service to the community. They have their own unique place in the world of work.

Of course, this is a broad continuum. There are organizations all along the spectrum that I outlined.

As an example, there's a type of company called a "community foundation," which is something like a bank for non-profits.

Community foundations typically manage millions of dollars, and make financial grants to smaller organizations. You might place them somewhere in between the non-profit and middle-way sections of my diagram.

Certified "B Corps" which pledge to support social good are a type of for-profit company that also leans between sections. These companies aim to be profitable, but are committed to goals like environmental preservation and poverty alleviation. Ben & Jerry's ice cream and Patagonia clothing company are two of the most famous B Corps.

There are companies all along the spectrum. Let me give some examples of organizations that you might find at various points.

<u>For-Profit Companies</u>
Retail Stores
Hotels
Marketing Agencies
Banks
Manufacturers
Construction Firms
Engineering Companies
Airlines
Software Developers
Energy Companies

<u>Middle Way Organizations</u>
Hospitals
Police and Fire Departments
Health Care Companies
Universities
The Postal Service
K-12 Schools
Doctors' Offices

Military
Certified "B Corps" (for-profit)
Community Foundations (non-profit)

<u>Non-Profit Organizations</u>
Social Service Agencies
Museums
Environmental Protection Groups
Religious Institutions
Animal Welfare Organizations
Professional Associations
Group Homes for People with Disabilities
Food Banks
Literacy Groups
Youth Organizations

Take a look at the diagram above, or read through some of these samples, and try to get a sense of where you might like to be. See what attracts you at this stage of your life.

Does the thrill of helping to grow a business and develop a customer base appeal to you?

Or are you more interested in providing direct service to people and communities at low or zero cost?

Or does something in the middle seem appealing—working for an educational, health care, or government-funded group, for example?

Each of these has its own culture. As you may recall from my opening chapter, my first few jobs were at a computer store (for-profit), a road-paving company (for-profit, though serving local governments), an urban planning company (non-profit), and a manufacturer (for-profit). The missions, cultures, and styles at each of these companies were wildly different.

Try to get a sense of where you might like to explore. You can always explore something else in the future; we're just focusing on your immediate steps. But see if there's a place on this continuum that feels interesting to you.

Third Question: Size

The next question I ask my clients is one that I have rarely seen on a career assessment—although I find it important.

It is a simple question, but one that can make a world of difference on your journey through the world of work. It is this:

"How large of an organization would you like to work for?"

The difference between a 5-person company, a 500-person company, and a 5000-person company is enormous.

At small companies, there is often much more chaos than at large companies. There usually aren't established systems in place. Most employees wear "multiple hats"—they do more than one job every day. There are frequently staffing and cash flow challenges. Speed is essential, and when speed conflicts with quality, speed generally wins.

Personally, I love small companies. I enjoy the rough-and-tumble, order-from-chaos challenges. I love the entrepreneurial feel of things. I enjoy making a direct, immediate impact on the company direction. But I know many people who can't stand this type of environment.

Very large companies, by contrast, usually have a completely different culture. Large companies generally have established systems. Professionality is one of the most valued qualities. Each employee is generally an expert in her or his realm; you can settle on "one hat" to wear, and you can wear that proudly. Quality is more important than speed.

Many people enjoy the stability and established structure of large corporations. They appreciate having systems to protect the integrity of the workplace. They don't mind the bureaucracy, because they understand that it's designed to catch and protect against errors. They enjoy not having to worry about the financial viability of the organization. I've spoken to many people who only want to work for large corporations.

Here's an interesting statistic about company size: 99% of companies in the United States are "small" businesses (less than 500 employees). And yet, the other 1% of "large" businesses actually employ half of all people.

So essentially, there's a 50-50 split between people working for large and small companies. Many of the large businesses have thousands of employees spread across the world. Some of the small companies only have one or two employees. The culture, speed, values, and goals are vastly different in small and large organizations.

So let me ask you: What size company might you be interested in working for?

Does a scrappy, speedy, sometimes-chaotic small organization appeal to you?

Or do you like the order and stability of a large organization?

Most non-profit companies are small, though there are some large national ones as well. For-profit companies range from tiny to huge. Middle-way organizations—schools, hospitals, government groups, and so forth—are similarly diverse in size.

No matter where you are on the profit/non-profit continuum, you can find large or small organizations to join. The choice is up to you.

Fourth Question: Environment

The next question that I often ask my clients is about work environment.

Let me return to my own job examples. My first job was at a store, where I roamed around the building during my shift. I then worked on a road crew, outside, driving a truck on occasion. My next two jobs were "desk jobs," where I sat at a computer all day in an air-conditioned office.

Even though I'm a computer guy, I actually disliked the desk-job format. I prefer to be moving around. Even today, I'll go from bouncing on an exercise ball at my desk, to working at a coffee shop for hours, to walking while taking calls on my headset. I personally like the flow of motion.

Other people are different. Some prefer to have a stable workstation in a comfortable environment. Others like to be outdoors all day. There are those who enjoy driving vehicles. Some people prefer working from home.

There are people who love to work on academic campuses, at airports, or in warehouses. Some people enjoy field-based work. There are folks who like to travel extensively, and then there are others who will do almost anything to avoid travel of any sort.

I invite you to think about this question:

"What type of work environment appeals to you?"

Let me share two examples of folks who explored very different environments.

One of my favorite plumbers started his career as an IBM mainframe computer programmer. But he didn't like sitting at a computer all day, so he took a new job working with a highway construction company. He eventually switched from that to plumbing, and now his job is to train new plumbers in the trade. He found a work environment that he liked, through experimentation.

A friend whom I referenced earlier graduated from law school and set up a criminal defense practice in California. He ran a successful business until there came a day when he "couldn't stand the sight of his carpet." He had grown tired of the work, the environment, and everything else. He soon developed a new career as a musical performer at libraries, schools, and children's parties. He found a creative new work-environment fit.

You too can choose among a nearly limitless array of work environments: offices, schools, hospitals, stores, trucks, docks, homes. The list is almost endless.

Let me ask you: What type of work environment appeals to you? Mostly indoor or mostly outdoor? Desk-based or in motion? Do you prefer a single work site, or might you like being at a different place each day? Try to get a sense of what attracts you.

There's another dimension to work environment that I invite you to consider: social contact level. Do you like having a lot of people around you—customers, coworkers, and the general public? Or do you prefer to be left alone to do your work?

You can combine any of these environmental factors as you wish.

A small farmer, for example, is generally working outdoors without a lot of social contact.

A policewoman might be outdoors like the farmer, but with almost endless interpersonal contact.

A computer programmer will be indoors, often with limited interruptions from other people.

A retail store worker will be indoors with a great deal of social interaction.

"I'm really not sure about any of this!" some people say.

If you're feeling that way, it's completely understandable. The many options can be daunting. That's why it's so important to actively explore different environments. Feel free to chat with friends who work in different settings, and ask them how they spend their days. Volunteer or ask to "shadow" workers in a non-profit setting.

Above all, keep your eyes open as you go through your life—when you're at a restaurant, getting your car serviced, renewing your driver's license, or anything else. Look around at what people are doing. What is the environment like? Is there energetic motion, or calm stability? Is there a lot of social interaction, or little? How might it feel to work in that type of setting?

As I mentioned earlier, I used to study *What Do People Do All Day?* until the book binding broke. I still like to peek around work environments. What is going on in the kitchen of that cafe? What do those clerks do when they're on break? How much time does that tow truck driver have between jobs? It's fascinating to observe.

Our economy is constantly changing; I find myself continually exposed to unique jobs that I never knew existed. A pre-flight printing specialist. A chemometrician. A UI/UX designer. A takeoff construction estimator.

Even career counselors can't keep track of all the new career paths arising each year. Because of that, a good strategy is to follow your inner pull toward general areas that interest you, and then observe and ask people in those fields questions.

Most people will be delighted to share insights about their work. I've personally had numerous people—including children in school—email me with questions about what it's like to be a counselor and psychotherapist. I've also had people ask me what a recruiter does. I'm always happy to answer questions, especially brief ones via email.

Let me wrap up this section with one last question that I ask my clients.

Fifth Question: Work Investment

This last question ties in to issues of work-life balance, family, finances, and many other personal goals. It is this:

> **"How much of your day-to-day life do you want to give to your work?"**

I've received the widest variety of answers to this question.

Some people say, "I want to give hardly *any* of my life to my work, of course!"

Other people say, "My work is my life. I don't know what to do with myself when I'm not working."

Most people say something like, "Work is important to me, but so are my family and hobbies and other things. I want a balance."

There is no right answer to this question. But it's an important one to think about.

Returning to my first question, about self-employment: If someone tells me that they want to pursue self-employment, but then on this fifth question they tell me that they want to give as little as possible to their work, that's a bit of a red flag.

A few people do start a business, "get rich quick," and exit. But that's rare.

Instead, most self-employed people are devoted to their work. They invest their hearts in their offerings, and often they're engaged with their businesses around the clock.

The same is true for many teachers, doctors, social workers, and other helping professionals. Managers and executives are often "on the clock" constantly. Artists, musicians, writers, and other creative types tend to put a great deal of themselves into their work.

Technical people can be the same. One of the first software programmers I placed in my recruiting work would go to the office, put in his eight hours developing software, and then go home and develop even more software for a side business of his. He lived in the world of software. It was the focal point of his life. He loved it, and immersed himself in software development from morning until night.

"That sounds ridiculous!" you might be thinking. "Who wants to work around the clock?"

If that's how you feel, you're in good company. Most people appreciate their work, and enjoy the contributions they make. But their real focus in life may be time spent with their families or communities. Volunteer opportunities may be important to them. They are seeking a balance between work and personal life.

I've talked to other people who are eager to stop working completely. These people are usually passionate about non-work activities, including sports, personal growth, or hobbies. Many of them are saving money in the present in order to retire early. Some are skilled investors and are planning to transition out of the work world as soon as their finances allow.

None of these are good or bad. I myself have been in all three of these modes at various points in my life. All three of these types can have extremely fulfilling careers.

So let me ask you: At least at the present time, how much of your day-to-day life would you like to invest in your work?

Would you like a career path where you have the freedom to climb mountains or go surfing whenever you like?

Or would you like your work to fuse with the rest of your life so fully that you can't tell where one ends and the other begins?

Or is there a balance that appeals to you? Perhaps a career where you can work for four or eight hours a day, and then put work aside completely in order to spend time with your loved ones?

Again, there is no right answer to this. But it is an essential question, and it can be an important determiner of a good career match.

You'll notice that my five questions didn't include, "How much money do you want to earn?"

I do get around to that question with my clients, but only after getting a sense of their deeper interests, values, and goals.

Here's why I don't prioritize income discussions: In almost every field, there are roles that earn a great deal of money and roles that earn far less.

For example, let's take the banking industry. The difference in income between a commercial bank teller and a director at an investment bank is enormous. One may make hundreds of times as much as the other. Both roles are in banking, but the income difference is significant.

Similarly, wages for manufacturing assemblers and technicians can range from minimum-wage to six-figure incomes. I've met folks in the skilled trades who are earning an enormous amount, and those who are just scraping by.

There are some career paths, including many in sales, where you start out earning a very modest amount and then quickly progress to robust compensation packages.

So no matter what career path you choose, there will likely be many ways to pursue your income goals—goals that may change over the course of your life. I encourage you not to over-weight that factor when you're choosing a field to explore.

At this stage, the goal is simply to follow your inner compass to seek out directions that interest you.

Exploration

So having considered these five questions, what now?

Now begins the active exploration process. As I mentioned earlier, this is not something that can be done by reading a book or taking an assessment. Career exploration is a highly action-based process.

To return to the vacation example at the start of this chapter: Our person decided to go to a rainforest for her vacation. That helped her to narrow the options significantly. But now she can begin to explore. What rainforests are there, in which countries? What are the lodging options? What are the key sights to see?

She will have fun investigating things. She might read reviews. She might look at videos. She might reach out to people who have visited the areas she's considering, and ask them about their experience. The focusing questions pointed her to an area that she can actively dive into further.

So it is with career exploration. Perhaps you answered the five questions, and decided that you'd like to explore the non-profit world. Or small, entrepreneurial companies. Or jobs at universities. Or work at an airport. Now is the time to actively investigate those possibilities. The investigation can take place through research, conversations, and real-life observations.

In addition, it may be helpful to read through *lists of jobs* in your areas of interest to get the wheels turning.

I find that job lists are the most interesting thing about career assessments. It's fun to go through them with people, simply to see what their reactions are.

A forest service ranger? A videographer? An excavator operator? An occupational therapist? Do any of those catch your interest, and why?

To help you with this, I've included a series of career and job lists at the back of this book organized into groups. Feel free to browse through those and see if any catch your eye.

I have included hands-on jobs, and jobs that can be done remotely; jobs for people who like words, and others for those who like numbers; jobs that involve travel and jobs that involve food. As you read through those, see which evoke a pull to explore further.

Let me also recommend an excellent free resource. The O*NET OnLine website at www.onetonline.org is run by the U.S. Department of Labor, and lists thousands of jobs organized by field.

If you browse through the "Government & Public Administration" section, for example, you'll find everything from agricultural inspectors to infantry soldiers to court clerks to tax examiners. I will discuss the O*NET OnLine resources further in the Q&A section that follows this chapter. I highly recommend using it.

Beyond lists, consider asking people about their work. Let them know that you're considering a move into their field and are curious about what it's like. Ask them if it's OK to pose a few questions. Social network sites like LinkedIn and Facebook can be great places to find folks to reach out to (some of whom might be connected to friends of yours.)

As I mentioned, I've had numerous people ask me what it's like to do the work that I do. I've always been happy to give some answers. Other people are very likely to answer questions for you as well.

Recap and An Example

To conclude this chapter, let me recap the five questions I've outlined. I'll then share an example of how I use these in conversations with clients.

In the next chapter, I'll take a deeper look at the process of career exploration, and offer some additional techniques and approaches. These five questions are just a start; I encourage you to dive deeper after you've considered them.

The five questions are:

1. Are you interested in working for an existing company, or would you prefer to be self-employed?
2. Do you feel attracted to the for-profit world, the non-profit world, or perhaps something in the middle?
3. How large of an organization would you like to work for?
4. What type of work environment appeals to you?
5. How much of your day-to-day life do you want to give to your work?

Let me now share a brief example of how I might use these in a counseling session.

Imagine that a client named Nathan comes to see me. He's seeking a more fulfilling career path.

"So Nathan," I say, "you're looking for something more fulfilling than what you've been doing. Do I understand that correctly?"

"Yeah," he says. "My jobs have been sort of meaningless. I want to do something that matters."

I ask him, "Are you thinking about working for an established organization, or is self-employment something you're considering?" [Q1]

"Self-employment? Wow. That would be great. Do you think that's possible?"

"Sure," I say, "but let me ask a couple questions about self-employment. Would you be OK being in sales mode a lot of the time—at least at the beginning?"

"Oh goodness. I hate sales."

"OK. What about income that ebbs and flows? Would you be comfortable if you didn't have much income flowing at the beginning?"

"I really need something stable," he says.

"OK, my guess is that self-employment might not be the ideal path for now. We can return to that in a bit, but let's assume that you need a steady paycheck."

"Yeah, that sounds good."

"From your resume, it looks like you've only worked at for-profit companies. Are you thinking about non-profit work? Or perhaps something in the middle like education, health care, or government organizations?" [Q2]

"That last one sounds interesting. What would it be like to work for the government?"

"Well, there are different levels of the government from federal to state to local, and each of those has many groups. There's everything from national parks to the state department of revenue to local police and fire."

"I think I'd really like working for a government group. Probably more than working for a standard non-profit."

"Great, we can discuss that further. Now, I see that you've worked for some big companies. Do you prefer a large organization or a small one?" [Q3]

"I'm pretty neutral. I can go either way on that."

"Great. How about work environment. Do you like working indoors or outdoors? At a desk or moving around? And how much social interaction do you like?" [Q4]

"I'm pretty social. In fact, my last few jobs felt isolating. Indoors at a desk is fine, but I can also be out of the office. In fact, a blend might be nice."

"OK. Big last question. How much of your day-to-day life do you want to invest in your work? How much of your time and your heart do you want to give?" [Q5]

"I'd like to find something that will really grab me. Something that's an important part of my life. That's why I came to talk to you. I don't want a job where I just punch-in, punch-out on the clock. I want something really meaningful."

And now we have a fairly clear vision of where Nathan can explore further. I'm guessing that a government agency like child protection services might be worth discussing. Perhaps a county mental health organization will appeal to him. Or perhaps he'd like to work at a state employment agency, helping people to find jobs!

That conversation with Nathan only took a few minutes. But it helped to focus areas for further exploration. That is the goal of the five questions.

Now, there is something important I'll discuss with Nathan that I want to highlight here. It is one of the most essential ideas about careers that I share with my clients. It is this:

We bring meaning to our careers. Our careers do not bring meaning to us.

Nathan said that he's looking for "something that matters." But it's important for him to realize that *he himself* brings what matters to his work. Simply working for a government agency will not automatically give him a sense of meaning.

I have spoken to a large number of people who went into non-profit, social service, teaching, or health care careers who feel that their work is nothing but "a bunch of red tape," "a broken system," "a group of egocentric jerks," or any number of other colorful descriptors. I also know people who work for ordinary for-profit businesses and find deep meaning in their work.

Your career is a canvass upon which you paint. It is a stage upon which you act. It is a studio you fill with your creative activity. Your career is simply an avenue of expression.

That is why choosing a specific career is less important than choosing what you want offer the world *through* your career. I will discuss this dynamic in greater detail in the chapters to come.

For now, I'd like to underscore that no matter what you do for work, you can offer your gifts. No matter what your specific job is, you can bring helpfulness, wisdom, problem-solving abilities, and other offerings. As you offer your gifts through your work, you will very likely increase your sense of career fulfillment—no matter what you do.

Now, are there some careers in which your gifts will flow more easily? Certainly there are, and we want to find those.

But sometimes the best career development step is to focus on giving your gifts right where you are. That can open wonderful new paths. I'll return to this idea throughout this book.

For now, let me take a deeper dive into some of the themes in this chapter by offering a series of Q&As about the process of exploring careers. Many of these are common questions I've received from clients.

CHAPTER THREE

Exploring Career Paths: A Deeper Look

In the previous chapter, we looked at five questions that can help you focus your career exploration. I also suggested action steps like observing work environments, having discussions with people who work in fields you find interesting, and volunteering or shadowing.

In this chapter, I'll take a deeper look at various facets of the career exploration process. After that, the rest of this book will be focused on practical ways to move your work life forward.

I am a big believer that your career will unfold in its own unique, unpredictable way. Identifying one single path is far less important than moving forward wherever you feel a pull. Your career path will emerge as you take steps to follow your inner sense of what feels right for you.

I'll be using a Q&A format for this chapter, as these are common questions that I've received from clients, friends, and readers over the years.

Q: Your five questions seem like a good start. But I have absolutely no idea what careers are out there. Do you have any additional suggestions?

A: Sure. Let me offer an additional resource that you might find valuable, along with some career counseling history.

The O*Net Online website that I referenced earlier is a free resource and a helpful place to begin. Part of the website called the "Interest Profiler" at www.mynextmove.org/explore/ip is a 60-question assessment of your career interests. I recommend that you take this free assessment, and see what it suggests.

The O*NET Interest Profiler, like many other career assessments, is based on something called a "Holland code" framework developed by psychologist John Holland in the 1950s.

The Holland code framework divides the world of work into six groups, known by the acronym RIASEC:

1. "Realistic" people enjoy working with physical things.
2. "Investigative" people enjoy ideas, science, and the process of investigation.
3. "Artistic" people enjoy creative pursuits.
4. "Social" people enjoy social service and other helping activities.
5. "Enterprising" people enjoy leadership and entrepreneurial roles.
6. "Conventional" people enjoy information-oriented and organizational work.

No one is squarely in any one of the RIASEC camps; we all have blended interests that cross between these categories.

Part of the Holland code approach involves arranging RIASEC in a hexagon. When you do that, the adjacent letters (for example, Artistic and Social) tend to blend together more commonly than the opposite letters (for example, Artistic and Conventional).

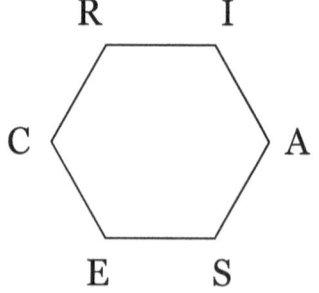

However, everyone is unique. Many people have unexpected blends.

As a personal example of this: When we practiced taking a Holland Code assessment in graduate school, everyone in the room found that their "Social" (helping careers) score was at the top. Everyone except for me. My Artistic score was by far the highest. My Investigative, Social, and Enterprising scores were all roughly tied for second place.

I took the O*NET Interest Profiler 15 years later, and lo and behold—I received almost the exact same result. So our interests can often remain remarkably stable through the years. My A-I-S-E combo probably explains why I enjoy writing and other creative pursuits, science and technology, and entrepreneurial activities along with helping and support roles.

Once you have established your RIASEC scores, the O*NET Interest Profiler will ask you to choose a "job zone" on a scale of one to five. Job zones indicate how much education, training, and preparation you are willing to invest in your work.

After that, the system spits out a series of career options for you to consider.

Now, as a test for this book, I just ran through the assessment (including all five job zones) to see what type of matches the system found for me.

Did it recommend a career as a counselor? Yes indeed! That was one of the top matches.

But how about a recruiter? Nope.

A human resources consultant? No.

An entrepreneur? No.

How about a book writer? Well, there was a mention of a "technical writer" in there, so I suppose that's in the ballpark.

The point is that computer-based systems can be hit-and-miss. They are not a substitute for real life exploration. The thing that I *do* like about these systems is that they can get the wheels turning in your mind with lists of jobs to consider.

If you click on "Find More Careers" after you've finished the O*NET Interest Profiler, the site will give you a large list of career paths. This can be a great imagination exercise.

An Industrial Ecologist? (What the heck is that?) An Urban and Regional Planner? (I did try that when I was seventeen.) An Investment Fund Manager? (My uncle actually does this...I could ask him for more information.) It's interesting to read through these and think about what each of them might involve.

I believe that your inner compass will "pull" you as you take action steps to explore various career paths. Assessments like the O*NET Interest Profiler, along with the resulting lists of fields, can be a helpful way to get the process started. You can read through these lists and note where you feel an interest pull.

I've also included a list of jobs and careers organized into groups at the end of this book. Feel free to browse through those, and then explore any interesting ones further.

Q: I have done a lot of different jobs and didn't like any of them. Should I keep looking? Or is it pointless to try to find something fulfilling?

A: I certainly support you in seeking happiness in your work, no matter what your past experience was.

I would need more information from you about your background, but let me share the following general response. If you have mostly worked in a specific field (for example, customer service or hospitality), you might want to try branching out to some new environments. My five questions, or the Holland code framework, may point you in a new direction to explore.

If you have worked in a variety of different roles, and you find that all of them are triggering the same experience in you, I'd put on my therapist hat and ask you a few questions.

What specifically did you not like about your jobs? Was there a common theme? I would be looking for patterns that might be unconsciously replicating.

Let me share an example of how this might look with a client. Let's call her Lara.

"So Lara," I say, "you didn't like any of your recent jobs. Can you pick one of them and tell me the worst part of it?"

"Sure," says Lara. "I worked at an office as an admin. It was just paper shuffling all day. Filing things, filling out forms. Completely unfulfilling."

"OK, tell me about another job."

"I worked in a restaurant. It was fun at first, but you get tired of just taking orders and bringing out plates of food, you know? I had enough after a while."

"Got it. Can you give me one more job example?"

"Yeah, I tried sales for a while. I actually worked selling used cars, if you can believe that. It just wasn't for me. All that mattered to the company was hitting the numbers, week after week."

Now, Lara has given me three data points. She has worked three very different types of jobs, but the common theme is that she gets tired of the repetitive, tedious elements of each. My guess is that she has not been intellectually or creatively challenged in any of her roles. She might flourish in an environment in which she tackles new, difficult projects each day.

I might talk to her about technical positions like software development. Or creative roles like marketing. Or perhaps she'd be open to self-employment, which will likely offer an endless amount of new challenges. Perhaps she would like to explore a management role—either management of people, or project management.

If your experience is like Lara's, you might want to look at the common themes in your past roles.

Did you find your jobs boring? If so, you may need more challenges. You might consider seeking out additional training or education—both as a preparation for a new role, and also as an immediate intellectual pursuit.

Did you find your work cultures cold or uncaring? If so, you can seek out a warmer, friendlier organization. (They do exist!) This might be a non-profit, but it might be a well-run for-profit or middle-way company as well. You can often get a sense of a company's emotional culture during the interview process.

Do you find a 9-5 schedule constraining? If so, you might want to try something with a less structured workflow. Some realtors, for example, work primarily on weekends and evenings. "Per diem" medical professionals take temporary assignments as they wish, and then take time off. Many freelancers and consultants work in bursts throughout the week.

The world of work is vast. As you explore new fields, and try new things, you may be surprised to find what options appear. Exploration is essential.

Q: I have a hard time making changes. Whenever I find a new career that sounds interesting, I second-guess myself and end up staying where I am. What can I do about this?

A: Let me keep my therapy hat on for this question.

One of the core principles in cognitive behavioral therapy is that our *thoughts* influence our *emotions*. Usually when there are feelings of doubt, inhibition, and conflict during decision-making processes, there are a number of thoughts fueling those feelings.

If you find a career path that seems interesting, and then you start to feel inhibited about taking steps to explore that path, you can take a peek around your mind to see what thoughts are lurking there.

You might, for example, find thoughts like:

"Perhaps I should just stay with the job I have. It's not too terrible, and a new one might be worse."
"It's too much of a risk to try something new."

"I'll probably be disappointed with a new career if I try it."
"What if I try a new career and fail? That would be awful."

And so on.

When you find a thought that isn't supporting your career exploration process, you can use a psychological technique called "cognitive restructuring." Cognitive restructuring is just a fancy way of saying "thought swapping."

Try swapping in some new, de-pressuring, self-supportive thoughts. Thoughts like:

"Hey, I'm just exploring this new path. I don't have to make a commitment to it."
"If I try something new, and it doesn't work out, that's not the end of the world."
"If I apply for a job and get an offer, I don't have to take it. It's OK to just explore what's out there."
"This is just a learning process. I can have fun with it."

I have helped many of my clients to identify inhibition-producing thoughts, and then swap in new thoughts that re-frame the career exploration process in a less pressuring way. This is one of the reasons that I almost always blend career counseling with broader cognitive behavioral therapy.

I'll revisit this process in the following chapters. But for now, let me underscore the idea that exploring new careers can be fun. There is no pressure to take a leap into something new. You're just observing, exploring, and learning what's out there.

If you try a new career path, and find that it's not for you, well—you're in good company. Most of us have tried new things, found that they weren't an ideal fit, and then moved on to something else.

Removing a sense of pressure can help to ease the dynamic of second-guessing that often takes place during this process.

Q: There is a career I'm interested in, but I don't think I have the skills for it. Is it worth trying anyway?

A: I'm a big believer that skills can be developed—and that development of skills over time is more important than any innate talent.

Over the course of my work, I've been continually impressed by the capacity of people to develop new abilities and excel in new roles. As I mentioned earlier in this book, I've met people who made radical shifts of careers. These people needed to build up their skills and knowledge within the new fields, often from scratch. But they found the process rewarding.

I encourage you to explore careers that interest you, regardless of your assessment of your skill level. The exploration can't hurt. And it may turn out that you have far more aptitude in the new career than you realized!

Now, having said, that, let me share a few things to be aware of in the process.

If you're planning to enter into a career that requires new skills, you may need to spend time as a student, apprentice, or trainee. For months (or even years), you may be in "learning" mode.

In the skilled trades like plumbing or electrical work, there are often formal apprenticeship programs to help with this. I have chatted with several apprentices who were accompanying contractors working on my home. Some of these people had been bartenders; others had been in sales. Now, they are apprentices in learning mode, and they may be for quite a while. It's important to be comfortable with this learning process.

You may also consider starting in a role that requires less training while you pursue further education. For example, some nurses start their career paths as Certified Nursing Assistants (CNAs) or Medical Assistants (MAs). After a while they may choose to gain more education and become Licensed Practical

Nurses (LPN), or perhaps even Registered Nurses (RN) or Nurse Practitioners (NP). Each of those roles requires different levels of education and training.

As always, I encourage you to follow your own inner compass to explore careers that interest you—regardless of skill or education requirements.

Once you've identified some fields of interest, begin to research those fields and talk to people who work within them. You will get the best sense about the true requirements of the field from people who already work there.

Q: I know what I want to do for my career: watercolor painting. I can spend all day painting and never get bored. But I hardly make any money selling my art. How can I pursue this career?

A: I've worked with many creative professionals in my counseling practice, and this is a common question from people who are gifted at acting, singing, writing, and other artistic fields.

If you were my client, I would begin by exploring ways that you can use your watercolor skills in new contexts.

For example, might you consider working as a freelancer with marketing agencies or design studios? An agency might love to have a watercolorist create elements for larger pieces.

Would you be interested in creating a website and offering custom watercolor paintings for customers? Perhaps in a particular niche? Some artists create paintings from photographs of family portraits or pets.

Let's branch out further. Would you consider offering painting instruction, either one-on-one or via a class? Would you be willing to create instructional videos and post them online? This can help to spread the word about your work.

Might you consider a parallel career as an art teacher in a school? You can still paint your own pieces in parallel.

When I have these types of conversations with my creative clients, I usually find that one of two things happen.

Either my clients are excited to explore broader ways to use their skills, or they say, "Dan, I only want to practice my art in this one particular way."

I usually explore their resistance to creative expansion, and encourage them to adopt an open-minded, brainstorming perspective.

The conversation might look like this:

"So Martin," I say, "It sounds like none of the things we just talked about appeal to you."

"Painting pets, Dan? Totally kitschy. I'd rather quit painting than do something like that."

"OK. And helping a marketing agency—no go on that?"

"I don't want to use my paintings to sell things. That's not why I got into this."

"And what about teaching people how to paint?"

"Doubt it. I'm not patient enough."

"OK. I still believe that there are a number of ways you can use your talents while you continue to do fine art. Now, you're a creative guy—right?"

"I like to think so."

"OK, let's get creative here. Help me brainstorm a few ways that you can use your watercolor skills in a completely new way. Don't worry about money. Just try to come up with some new, creative ways that you can use your skills."

"OK, fine, I guess I could create some stuff for my girlfriend's jewelry-making business. She could use some help with her logo and whatnot."

"Great idea. Give me another."

"The homeless shelter I volunteer at sometimes does auctions. Maybe I could paint a few clients, if they gave permission. Then the shelter could auction the paintings."

"Brilliant. One more."

"Well, there's a farmer's market in town that lets artists sell their stuff. I was thinking about doing some around-town pieces that would fit in there."

And we're off to the races. For Martin, beginning to creatively open his mind was key.

He might find a patron at the farmer's market. The person who buys a piece at the fundraiser might want more of his work. The designs for his girlfriend's business might lead him to help other businesses with logo or website art.

I believe that if you explore new ways to use your talents with a very open mind, you'll find almost limitless avenues. Open-mindedness as you explore options is key.

Q: You talk about following your "inner compass" to explore career paths. However, I just don't seem to feel a pull in any direction. My compass seems broken. Is there anything I can do to fix it?

A: I don't believe that anyone's inner compass truly breaks. But I do believe that all of us have layers of interference that make it difficult to receive messages from our compass.

Let me share three "compass clearing" techniques that I use with clients in my sessions.

First Technique: Release Interfering Thoughts

The first technique, which I referenced above, is to identify and replace any thoughts that dampen a sense of enjoyment. The career discovery process can be like exploring a new land. It can be a fun and interesting process.

If career exploration *doesn't* feel like that, you may want to seek out any thoughts that inhibit that sense of enjoyment. Thoughts like:

"Why should this next job be any different. I've always disliked my jobs."

"Work is just about making money for someone else."

"There's too much competition out there. I'm not up for the battle."

You might find completely different thoughts. You'll have to search your own mind and see what is there.

When you find anything that is dampening your sense of exploratory enjoyment, you can use a thought swapping technique, and replace the old thought with a mind-opening new one.

The new thought can be something simple like:

"Hey—who knows what will happen if I research this career path? I can keep an open mind as I explore."

The goal is to clear the mind of interference, and enter into an open-minded state. From there, you might begin to feel the "pulls" more easily.

Second Technique: Hot and Cold

A second technique is to simply choose a path (at random, if need be) and begin to explore it. As you do that, try to get a sense of "hot or cold" like the children's game.

Let's say, for example, that you're not feeling a pull toward any particular path. So you go to the O*NET OnLine site that I referenced earlier, click randomly on lists of jobs, and come up with "Emergency Medical Technician."

An EMT doesn't seem to be a good fit for your interests, but that doesn't matter. We're going to use it as a starting point in our hot-or-cold game.

You begin with an exploration of the work life of an EMT. You learn about their schedules, their typical wages, and their responsibilities. You read a few articles written by EMTs about their work. You email the author of one of the articles, and ask her a few questions.

While you're doing that, you make a list of what you like and don't like about working as an EMT.

You don't like the idea of treating medical issues. That just isn't for you. But you do like the flexible schedule part. You also like the idea of helping people who are in danger.

You then use that to move forward. What are some other careers that have flexible schedules and involve helping people in danger, minus the medical treatment part?

Firefighters do that type of work, you realize. You explore the work life of a firefighter. You learn about wildland firefighters, who often work with forest fires. They even rappel out of helicopters at times. That sounds fascinating. You explore further.

And so on. In this approach, you choose a path (at random if need be), explore it, and ask yourself what elements you like and dislike. Then, like a hot and cold game, you move to related paths and explore those as well.

This can reduce any pressure to "find your one path." You're simply having fun exploring.

Third Technique: Involve Another Person

The third technique is to involve another person. This can be a counselor, of course. But it can also be a trusted, supportive friend or family member—someone who is committed to seeing the best in you.

You can ask that person, "What type of work can you envision me doing? What type of work do you think I would enjoy?"

You might be surprised at the insights you receive. Even if the person's feedback seems off base, you can add in the hot-and-cold technique I mentioned above.

"You could see me as an EMT? I actually really dislike medical treatment. Why did you think of me as an EMT? Because you could see me helping people in danger? That's interesting—yes, I guess I could see that too."

Dialogues like this can reveal some interesting things. And two minds working together create powerful synergies.

Q: I earned a graduate degree in a specific field. But after working in that field, I don't think it's for me. I worry that I may have wasted a lot of time and money. Do you recommend that I suck it up and just stay in my field?

A: This is a personal decision, and you'll have to follow your own sense of what's right for you. However, let me share a few ideas to think about.

Our work generally takes up a large part of the day. If you're in a field that doesn't feel right for you, you are effectively spending your day in a state of conflict. I don't recommend to any of my clients that they "suck it up" and simply tolerate distress.

Now, having said that, I do believe that careers are open containers for the expression of our gifts. If you were my client, I would discuss whether there were reorientations that you could make within your existing career.

Are there different roles you can try within your field? Are there different responsibilities that you can take on within your current job? Can you discuss career development opportunities with your supervisor? There may be many modifications that can be made.

However, if your inner compass is truly pointing you in a new direction, I encourage you to at least start an exploration process—regardless of whether you earned the "right degree" for the field.

I have worked with engineering technicians (and even a few engineers) who never completed an engineering degree. I have met software programmers who were entirely self-taught. I know addictions counselors who have certifications, but not counseling or psychology degrees. I've met doctors who went into business rather than medicine, lawyers who went into technical fields, and all sorts of other mash-ups.

Almost all of the people I'm thinking about are flourishing, regardless of any "mismatch" in degrees. So I wouldn't dwell on the idea that you made a mistake.

Very likely, you learned valuable things in the course of your study—things that can be applied to any new field that you explore. You might find it helpful to identify connections between your degree and any field that interests you, and imagine how you would describe those connections in an interview.

A nurse, for example, has social skills applicable to sales. A political scientist has analytical skills that can be used in a research lab. An IT support person has problem-solving skills that can be used at a non-profit.

If you look closely, you'll probably be able to find connections between *any* skill and *any* career field. This can be a great exercise, and may help you develop a further appreciation of the value of your degree.

Q: My husband wants to quit his job and use our savings to open a restaurant. He says it's his dream job. I'm not comfortable with him doing that. Is there anything I can say to him?

A: This can be a challenging dynamic. One partner wishes to follow his career dreams, and the other partner feels uncomfortable with the financial impact of that prospect. I imagine that every couples counselor has seen this type of situation.

Here is one option you can try: Let your husband know that you do want him to be happy in his work. But tell him that you want to make decisions cooperatively, in a way that works for both of you.

If he agrees to this, you can begin to creatively brainstorm action steps that are mutually comfortable. If he *doesn't* agree, then I recommend scheduling a session with a counselor. Almost every couples counselor will be able to assist you in making cooperative, mutually-agreeable decisions.

Let's assume that your husband is on board with finding an approach that you both are comfortable with. If that's the case, you can begin to explore some steps that will let him pursue his dream while simultaneously feeling workable to you.

For example, if I were working with you or your husband, I might ask questions like this to get the gears turning:

As a first step toward his dream, might your husband consider investing a small amount of money in an existing restaurant, and helping out there on the weekends? This might minimize the financial outlay, while exposing him to the day-to-day operations of running a restaurant.

Or might he consider opening a food service business that requires less financial investment than a full restaurant? Perhaps a food truck, a coffee shop, or a part-time catering service?

Would he consider seeking out investors so that he doesn't have to use your financial resources?

Would he be willing to focus on developing recipes, filing paperwork for the corporation, setting up a website, and other pre-opening activities? (I find that sometimes people's interests change as they begin to actually do this brass tacks work.)

The goal in this process is to find action steps that bring him happiness, and also feel comfortable to you. The questions above are just food for thought. You'll need to propose your own solutions, and solicit ideas from him.

Of course, you certainly have a right to say, "I'm not OK with you spending our money on a restaurant. No more discussion." However, I find that squelching someone's career dreams can create a great deal of resentment. It can create feelings of being trapped. It can spark a sense of hopelessness.

A far better approach is to seek solutions—even if they're small, initial, exploratory steps—that feel comfortable to everyone impacted.

Q: My adult son has no idea what to do for his career, and I want him to find something soon. What can I do to get him going?

A: This is the one of the most common questions I receive in my career counseling work. Here's how I usually respond:

I appreciate that you want to help your son. You might be worried that he hasn't found a fulfilling career path. You might even feel a bit frustrated with him, and want to give him a "push" in his career development process.

You can, of course, encourage him to schedule a session with a career counselor. Or you can give him a copy of this book, or any other number of career books. Or you can point him to the O*NET site that I referenced above. You can even join him in taking the O*NET Interest Profiler and have some fun comparing your results.

However, ultimately you will need to let him move at his own pace, in his own way. I have never seen someone who was being pressured by their family successfully engage with the career exploration process. It requires sincere, active involvement. If your son takes some steps solely due to pressure, he might land a job—but it's unlikely that he'll be in the mindset to discover a true career path.

Let me share an important observation about this type of situation.

When I planted ivy in my back yard, I was told that, "the first year it sleeps, the second year it creeps, the third year it leaps." It takes a couple of years for the ivy to build its root system. Things don't seem to be moving in the first or second years. But important work is going on underground. In the third year, it pops.

In a similar way, people who don't seem to be progressing in their careers may be learning essential skills and gathering knowledge. They might "leap" several years in the future, after their roots are stronger. It's essential to honor this process.

Now, are there people who are simply stuck? Certainly. For some people, there may not be a whole lot of root development occurring. This might be because of internal challenges like low self-confidence, or difficulties in the economy, or something else. These folks may benefit from receiving support from a counselor.

Other people, though, might be actively learning. I myself had several years in the early 2000s where I didn't seem to be accomplishing much. My recruiting clients were all in the middle of layoffs and downsizing after the dot-com bust. There simply wasn't much recruiting work to do.

In those years, I spent a great deal of time reading and writing. I had conversations with a wide variety of people at coffee shops. I moved to Colorado and took up rock climbing,

It may have seemed as though I was aimless. However, I was learning about cognitive behavioral therapy, which prepared me to go to graduate school a few years later. I was developing my relationship-building skills, which were weak at the time. I was clarifying some of my values and life goals. And I was developing my writing abilities. Plenty was happening under the surface.

Your son might also be engaged in a similar process. I encourage you to discuss his inner life with him. Despite outside appearances, he might be engaged in an active, growth-oriented process that will be essential for a future career path.

As always, I encourage communication.

Summary

Let me wrap up this chapter with a summary of the most important points I've covered so far.

Careers often evolve in unexpected and unpredictable ways. It's unlikely that you will travel along one fixed career path for your whole life. Your path is unique to you, and it will unfold in its own way.

You bring meaning to your career; your career does not bring meaning to you. You decide what to offer each day through your work activities. You decide what values to express, what goals to pursue, and how you want to be of help. Your career is simply an avenue for the expression of your abilities and gifts.

Having said that, there will certainly be career paths that are more suited to the expression of your particular gifts. I believe that your inner sense of what interests and "pulls" you is the best inner compass to follow as you explore different options.

You can begin the career exploration process by answering my five questions, taking the O*NET Interest Profiler, reading through job lists, visiting a career counselor, or any other number of approaches. However, the real work will involve actively investigating the fields that interest you. A helpful part of this process is communicating with people who are working in those fields. Many people will be very happy to answer your questions.

Career exploration can be enjoyable, like exploring vacation destinations. If you begin to feel stressed, inhibited, or pressured in the process, try to identify the thoughts that are contributing those feelings, and replace them with new, de-pressuring thoughts.

An attitude of, "Hey, I'm just exploring what's out there—there's no pressure to find a perfect match," is one of the best thoughts to travel with.

I will now move on to chapters focused on job seeking, resume writing, interviewing, self-employment, and improving your happiness at work. You're welcome to bounce ahead to whatever sections seem most relevant to your needs.

CHAPTER FOUR

The Job Search

You might be thinking, "OK Dan, I've found a career I'd like to try. But how do I find a *job* in that field?"

There are three primary ways to find new job opportunities. I will spend this chapter exploring each of these approaches in detail. Then, as I did in the last chapter, I will include a series of Q&As that will dive deeper into the process.

Please note that I will *not* be covering self-employment in this chapter. This section is for folks who are seeking roles with existing companies. If you're interested in setting up your own business, feel free to move right to chapter ten, which focuses on entrepreneurial activities.

Here are the three most common ways to find new work opportunities:

1. You can apply for jobs that are advertised.
2. You can make yourself visible so that recruiters like me can find you.
3. You can have conversations with people to learn about opportunities. Some people call this "networking."

"Ugg. Not networking. I hate that," many people say.

I'd encourage you to keep an open mind as you consider that third option, as up to *80%* of jobs are found through personal or professional connections.

The third method is extremely powerful. Plus, I'm going to offer an entirely new approach to the process that may appeal to you, especially if you find traditional networking distasteful.

Recall my early job stories from the start of this book. I landed my computer store job by walking into the store, introducing myself, and asking if they needed help. My chat with the salespeople on the floor opened the door. That falls into the "jobs through conversations" category.

My job with the road crew came when my mother asked an employee if they needed additional workers. My second stint with the paving company came when I saw the company in town and approached them. Neither of those jobs were advertised. Again, both of those came from the conversations category.

My internship with the regional planning company came through a friend of my family—another personal connection. Only my fifth job with the detergent company came through an advertised position that I applied for.

As I mentioned previously, direct conversations with people in your fields of interest can often open doors. Some people love to "matchmake," and those folks would be excited to help you get a job if there is a match to be made. Chatting with people might be all you need to do.

I'll explore career-oriented conversations in greater detail later in this chapter, including the new angle that I referenced.

For now, though, let me begin with a discussion of what most people associate with job searching: applying for jobs that are publicly posted.

First Avenue:
Posted Job Ads

Let me begin by stating that the key to a successful job search is keeping a *very open mind* throughout the process.

I cannot state this too strongly. As you read job postings and consider them, you will probably face a continual temptation to rule out what you're seeing. You mind will want to say, "not a fit, not a fit, not a fit."

This is completely normal. Most of my clients experience it. I myself experience it when I'm reading through resumes as a recruiter. The mind wants to reduce the complexity of the process by saying, "nope, nope, nope."

To maximize success, I encourage you to notice when that rule-out dynamic is happening and—despite any resistance—move in the direction of re-opening the mind. I will share some cognitive behavioral therapy techniques to help with this process in the Q&A section later on.

To illustrate this dynamic, here is a typical conversation I've had with many of my career counseling clients:

"Dan," my client says, "I spent the week looking through job postings like you suggested."

"And how'd it go?"

"Terrible. None of the jobs out there are a fit. I'm ready to give up."

"Tell me more."

"I look at the skills they need, and I never have them all. There aren't any good matches. Nothing is a fit."

"You probably remember that I work as a recruiter during the day," I say.

"Yeah."

"Well, I write some of those job ads. And I can tell you that in twenty years, I have never found a single person who matches everything on a job description."

"So how can you tell if you're close enough?"

"Often you can't tell," I say. "If you seem to be in the ballpark, and are interested in the job, I recommend that you apply and see how it plays out. The elements that don't match might be the *least* important to the company."

"But what if it says that certain skills are required?"

"Sure," I say, "those may be essential. However, when I write job descriptions, I often have a group of people giving me big lists of requirements. After a few interviews, many of the 'required' skills become 'nice to have.' If you feel that you're in the ballpark for a job, I recommend that you send in an application, highlight the matches, and let the company sort through things."

Now, some clients are OK with this. Others keep looking for a near-perfect match with a job description.

When those clients finally find a match and apply, they often don't receive a response and feel very discouraged. After weeks of looking, they found a great fit on paper. But for whatever reason, the real-life match didn't happen.

Because of that, I encourage you to apply for any roles that you find interesting—as long as you're *in the ballpark*. It's not in your best interest to waste energy second-guessing what the company may or may not be prioritizing.

Please also know that during the hiring process, I'm having a parallel conversation with my corporate clients.

I'm saying to them, "Just because this candidate's resume doesn't fit every bullet on the job description, it doesn't mean that she won't be a great fit. Let's keep an open mind and interview her. Perhaps there will be great interpersonal chemistry. Let's just invite her to interview, and see how it plays out."

Again, open-mindedness is key. It's key for job-seekers, and key for employers. Much of my day is spent encouraging both parties in this process to drop their preconceived notions and approach potential relationships with an open mind.

In the next chapter, I'll talk about how to structure your resume in order to make potential matches pop. But for now, I want to encourage you to simply maintain an open-minded attitude when you're looking through job descriptions.

If you feel fatigued or overwhelmed in the job search process, that's perfectly normal. Almost everyone experiences that.

Reading through hundreds of job ads can be exhausting. Both job applicants and recruiters frequently become information-overloaded. At those times, the mind will try to short-circuit the process by saying, "Not a fit, not a fit, not a fit."

Notice when that type of fatigue hits. Take a break when that happens, and allow the mind to calm, rest, and relax. Then, when you're ready, approach the job search again with as much open-mindedness as possible.

Know that we HR folks are trying to do the same thing from our side of the table.

Finding Ads

Let's now tackle where to find job openings. There are four main locations in which jobs are posted:

1. General job sites like Indeed, LinkedIn, and Monster.
2. Specialty job sites aimed at specific fields or groups.
3. Company web sites.
4. Government web sites.

In addition, there are nearly endless "aggregator" sites that collect and re-post jobs that were originally featured at these four sources.

Each of these four type of sites can be fertile ground for a job search. I encourage you to explore all of them.

As a recruiter, when I have a conventional job I'm trying to fill, I often start by posting job ads on the *general* sites. Positions like administrative assistants, sales professionals, accountants, and so forth are commonly featured on places like Indeed, LinkedIn, and Monster.

However, when I have a niche job that I need to fill, I often post an ad on a *specialty* site as well. For example, I've recruited many optical engineers over the years. When I have an opening for a job like that, I may turn to the Optical Society of America (OSA) job site, or the Society of Photo-Optical Instrumentation Engineers (SPIE) career center. These specialty job sites cater specifically to optical engineers.

I wish that more job seekers would visit those types of sites! If you're in a field (or part of a group) that has a specialty jobs site geared toward your background, please keep an eye on postings on that site. You may be one of a small group of people who see those ads. Specialty job posting sites exist for veterans, teachers, people in skilled trades, and many other groups.

Specific company websites are another important source of jobs. Although general sites like Indeed often repost jobs from company websites, a large number of job postings are missed. I always encourage my clients to bookmark the "careers" web page of specific companies that are interesting, and manually check postings every week.

A bonus of manually checking a company's website is that you get the most up-to-date read of which positions are still open. When we recruiters fill a position, we usually delete the job listing from our company's website immediately. Paid job ads, on the other hand, are often set to expire on their own after a month or two. Some ads on general job sites might be highlighting positions that were filled a few weeks ago.

Many large organizations—including universities and health care companies—feature hundreds of jobs on their own sites. Some of these jobs will not show up elsewhere. I encourage you to regularly visit the career pages of any companies, institutions, or organizations that catch your eye.

Finally, there are government sites. Let me be the first to admit that it can be challenging to search for government jobs.

There are many different levels of government, each of which has its own job site. Many government jobs are not featured on general sites or caught by the aggregators. Therefore, you'll need to do some searching.

This searching process can actually be a good thing; the harder it is to find a job posting, the fewer applicants there will be. Your research skills will help you stand out!

Let me give an example of the levels of government.

When I have a career counseling client in Boulder, Colorado who wants to explore government jobs, I encourage them to visit:

1. The city of Boulder website.
2. The county of Boulder website, which is a different organization than the city.
3. The state of Colorado website, which only lists state funded jobs—even though some of these jobs might be located in Boulder.
4. The federal government jobs website at USAjobs.gov, which has no connection or overlap with any of the previous three levels. Jobs with the National Forest Service, the IRS, the armed forces, the Environmental Protection Agency, or any other federal group will be posted here, even if they're in Boulder.

So there are four levels to explore: city, county, state, and federal.

In addition, I'll encourage my clients to visit government job sites for all *neighboring* cities and counties. Depending on commuting distance range, this may involve an additional 10 to 20 sites!

This can feel like an overwhelming and complex maze. However, as I mentioned, the harder it is to find these job postings, the fewer applicants there will be.

You can treat the process like an exploration game. When you stumble upon a somewhat-hidden job post, you've found something valuable. Few people want to engage in the hunt. You can find openings that others may miss.

Building a Habit

As I stated earlier, one of the greatest challenges in the job search process is overcoming fatigue and information overload. It's important to pace yourself, and not allow your mind to become overwhelmed by the many options.

Let me share a recommendation to help with this.

It is a recommendation that almost every one of my clients resists at first, despite how strongly I pitch it.

It is this:

Treat your job search process like brushing your teeth. Set aside a few minutes each day to look through job ads, just like you set aside time to brush your teeth. Keep things simple, easy, and routine.

Each day, schedule a few minutes to browse through job ads and perhaps send a resume off to one of them. Then stop for the day.

The next day, do it again. Then again the next day.

You're forming a habit as you do this. Don't allow yourself to over-extend yourself, or "push through" stress or overwhelm. Instead, take small, regular steps each day.

This is completely opposite from how most people approach job searching. Most people plunge into a job search with anticipation. They eventually find a job that sounds great. They send off an application and excitedly wait to hear back. After several weeks of not receiving a response, they become very discouraged and give up on the process.

I have spent an *enormous* amount of time encouraging my clients not to do this. We want to minimize the roller-coaster of emotions. We want to focus on the relaxed formation of a habit.

To help with this, I encourage my clients to write down their daily job search steps on a sheet of paper. We call this a "practice record" in cognitive behavioral therapy, and it can help to strengthen new habits.

THE JOB SEARCH

A practice record can look as simple as this. (I've included a link to a blank one at the end of this book.)

Monday	Tuesday	Wednesday	Thursday	Friday
Spent 5 minutes looking through jobs on Indeed. Saved one job.	10 minutes looking at nursing job site. Nothing of interest.	5 minutes looking on LinkedIn. Saw one interesting job. Saved it for tomorrow.	10 minutes applying to job from yesterday.	10 minutes looking through my college alumni job posting site. Nothing of interest.

You can limit your steps to just a few minutes at a time. 5 to 15 minutes a day, as the person did in the example above, form a powerful new habit and move things along nicely.

As absurd as it might sound, you can even scale back to just *one single minute a day* if you'd like. But actually do that one minute of job searching every day. Let it be the basis for a new habit.

To underscore this, let me share a conversation that I've had numerous times in my counseling sessions.

"So Adrianne," I say to my client, "how did the job search steps go this week?"

"Well," says Adrianne with a sheepish grin, "You're not going to like this, but I actually didn't do anything on my job search this week."

"That's fine," I say. "No rush from my side! However, I'm curious what made it challenging to take some steps."

"Well, I want to be in the right headspace."

"And you didn't feel that you were ready."

"Yeah. I didn't want to force anything."

"OK, would you be willing to try an experiment this week? Perhaps we can have you do a tiny step each day, even if you're not really feeling it. Even something simple like bookmarking one job site each day. Would you be OK with that?"

"I'm not sure that a tiny step will help me get a job," says Adrianne.

"What tiny steps will do," I say, "is help the mind feel more comfortable with the process. After a week or two of tiny steps, you might find that you're ready for bigger steps. If you're up for it, I'd recommend taking just one minute a day over the next week and track your steps on the practice record."

Now, something very interesting happens when I encourage people to engage in job search steps for a single minute each day.

Some clients of mine come back the next week and report on how the practice worked. We begin to build on that traction.

Other clients, however, come back and say, "Dan, you won't believe it, but I couldn't even do a single minute a day! I can't understand it!" Suddenly, I have an opening as a psychotherapist to explore resistance that is getting in the way: fears, conflicting wishes, or any other subconscious elements that may be inhibiting the forward progress.

I share this because I encourage you to set a manageable (even absurdly manageable) daily goal for your job search—five minutes, or just one minute—and track your progress each day. If you find that even one minute each day is too much, you may want to explore what is inhibiting your progress.

Feel free to choose anything for your daily job search practice: browsing job ads, bookmarking job sites, proofreading your resume, filling out an application, or anything else. Establishing momentum is the key.

If you encounter minimal resistance in this process, and are able to spend twenty or thirty minutes each day looking through job ads and sending off an application or two—great! You're well on your way. Thirty minutes a day is probably enough time for most people, if it becomes a daily habit.

Let me now share some recommendations about seeking and reading the job ads that you find.

THE JOB SEARCH

Seeking and Reading Ads

As I mentioned, I write the types of ads you'll be seeing. Most of the time, job ads are ideal "wish lists." Often ads are a mish-mash of *multiple* people's wish lists. No candidate will hit every element. Please don't let yourself feel discouraged if you don't find any perfect matches.

Instead, simply browse through ads, notice what you find interesting, and consider sending in an application to any position openings that may be in the ballpark.

No one in the HR world will be upset if you apply for a job that isn't a tight-enough match. Instead, most of us recruiters will be happy that you're on our radar in case we have a similar position in the future—or in case the position definition changes during the hiring process.

We are grateful that you are expressing an interest in our role. You are doing us a favor by applying. We know how much time and work it takes to submit an application. On behalf of the HR world, I want to say thank you.

"Dan, you've got to be kidding me!" you might be thinking. "I've talked to recruiters who don't care about me in the least! They treat me like I'm just a cog in a wheel."

You're right, of course. There are folks like that. But there are also recruiters like me who are honored that you are interested in our job openings.

The people who don't value you are probably not long for the world of recruiting and human resources. When they move on to other things, their replacements might see an old application of yours and give you a call.

The reason I share this is that I want to encourage you to shift your perspective if you're worried about applying for jobs that aren't a perfect fit. Many companies will be grateful that you are interested in helping them, even if there isn't a match for an immediate opening.

I appreciate every applicant who has taken the time to express interest in one of my roles. I keep *every one of them* in mind for other opportunities that may be a better fit. I have filled many openings by contacting applicants that had applied for a different job in the past. This happens all the time in the recruiting world.

Three Do and Don't Tips

Let me return to the statement I made at the beginning of this chapter: The most important thing you can do in your job search is to keep your mind open as you read through ads.

Along those lines, let me offer three tips to help expand your options:

1. When you're looking through job ads, search for unique keywords that may appear in the body of the ad. Don't only search on standard job titles.

Let's say that you've spent your career working in sales. If you search only on ads that contain the word "sales" in the title, you may miss out on roles like "Account Manager," "Business Development Specialist," "Customer Experience Liaison," and other uniquely titled roles.

To find relevant job opportunities, it's best to search on multiple keywords. I recently had a conversation with a friend who is seeking a role in marketing communications. I encouraged her to search on a variety of unique keywords like "collateral" (as in marketing collateral), "InDesign" (a common design layout program), "copy" (as in copywriting), and so forth.

If you search only for conventional titles, you might miss a number of ads, especially those from companies that use creative and unusual titles. It's best to include a wide variety of keywords in your search.

2. Bookmark a variety of job-posting sites and visit them regularly. Don't only rely on automated email "alerts" from the larger sites to send you jobs.

Email alerts for new jobs are great, of course. By all means, sign up for them. It's wonderful to have job openings arrive directly into your mailbox.

However, I recommend that you also regularly visit a variety of job sites that you've bookmarked. If you search on multiple keywords, as I recommended above, you'll probably want to do that via a manual search. Otherwise, your email box will become overloaded with alerts.

When clients of mine are engaged in a job search process, they often bring a laptop into our sessions so that we can bookmark job sites. I then encourage my clients to rotate through those sites every few days. Government job sites on Monday. University sites on Tuesday. Health care companies on Wednesday. And so on.

Almost every time a client has told me, "I can't find any job openings," I have been able to help them identify a number of job sites that they hadn't visited. There are always new possibilities to consider.

You can create a strong foundation for your job search by remaining open-minded as you bookmark sites—including smaller sites you might not have thought about at first. Then, as you form a habit of checking these sites regularly, you'll be covering a great deal of ground.

3. Stretch to open your mind as you consider which opportunities may be in the ballpark. Don't give in to "not a fit, not a fit, not a fit" mental patterns.

I've covered this repeatedly, but let me discuss it one last time. Occasionally, my career counseling sessions go like this:

"So Dorian, you said you would love to work with cars. What do you think of this ad for a mechanic?"

"Nah Dan, mechanic jobs are terrible."

"Really?"

"Yeah, my cousin is a mechanic. He hates it."

"But you said that your goal was to work with cars. And it looks like this company will do training."

"I trust my cousin. He says to stay away from mechanic jobs."

"OK, how about this ad for a customer service person at a garage? You could still work around cars, but you wouldn't be a mechanic."

"It's probably like being a mechanic."

"OK. How about this job with the city doing work on the buses?"

"Sounds like mechanic work."

And so on. You can see the resistant mind frame that Dorian is in. If he's willing to open his mind a bit, he will likely begin to see things differently. I might say to him:

"Dorian, would you be willing to do an experiment with me? Just for the next week, forget everything your cousin or anyone else has told you. Try to clear your mind completely. Then print me out three car-related job ads that seem like the best ones out there. Don't worry if they're a great fit. Just print them and bring them to our session for us to discuss."

If Dorian shows up for our session with his three ads, we will hopefully be able to crack things open a bit.

I'll be curious about what he liked from the ads he brings. At the very least, it will help me understand his psyche better, and suggest some better alternatives. Doing this exercise will hopefully bridge him from a "no, no, no" mindset into a more solution-oriented place.

In the same way, you might find it helpful to stretch your own open-mindedness as you look through ads.

You can try what I did with Dorian: You can print out one job ad each day, and identify the pieces that you liked from each job description. Then use those pieces to expand your keyword searches for tomorrow.

You might even consider taking a leap and sending off an application to one of the closest fits you printed off. It might turn out that the job is a bit different from what you originally envisioned.

Let me conclude this job ad section by saying once again that I know how tiring it is to read through hundreds of job ads.

I also know how disappointing it can be to find a job that seems like a great fit, and then not hear back from the company. I have experienced this myself, and I have also experienced it with numerous clients. You have my deep respect for your willingness to keep moving ahead, despite these feelings.

Job seeking can be fatiguing. That's why I recommend that you take regular, easy, relaxed steps each day. Neither job seeker nor employer knows when there will be a match, or how long the search process will take. That is why patience, comfortable pacing, and open-mindedness are so important.

Second Avenue:
Becoming Visible to Recruiters

Applying for posted job ads was the first option in your job search. Making yourself visible so that recruiters like me can find you is a second approach that can be helpful.

You might be thinking that you will never be contacted by a recruiter—that recruiters only focus on tech workers, executives, or other groups. However, that is not necessarily true, especially during tight labor markets.

As a recruiter, I proactively reach out to people for *every single one* of my job openings. I do this through networking, cold-calls, resume database searches, and other methods. I have contacted assemblers, accountants, administrative assistants, salespeople, office managers, and all sorts of other people.

No matter what field you're in, or what level of seniority you are at, you can expand your job search options by making yourself visible. Let us recruiters do some of the work for you!

The most direct way to signal to recruiters that you're open to new opportunities is to post your resume online—on Indeed, LinkedIn, Monster, or any of the specialty career sites in your field.

Of course, there are pros and cons of posting a resume. Let's consider them carefully before you make a decision about this.

Posting Your Resume: Pros and Cons

The biggest risk of posting your resume is that your current employer might see it and conclude that you're planning to leave your position. This can cause ripple-effects, both harmful and helpful.

If your employer sees that you've posted your resume, they might assume (correctly or not) that you're unhappy in your current role and are preparing to quit your job. They might begin to prepare for your departure. They might even start an active search for your replacement.

Or, alternatively, your employer might see your resume and talk to you about increasing your job satisfaction. They might ask if there is anything they can do to improve your happiness at work. This might end with you receiving a pay increase or promotion!

I have seen both of these ripple-effects, and others.

At the extreme negative end of things, I have heard of companies who are prepared to fire any employee who is seeking a new job. Personally, I think this is a self-destructive response. But you should know that there are employers out there who will terminate the employment of any active job-seekers.

Because of the potential impact on you, I recommend that you consider *very carefully* if you feel comfortable having your employer see your resume. Even if you try to post your resume confidentially, many employers can read between the lines and recognize details. Always assume that you may be identified.

This might not be an issue for you. Perhaps you are between jobs. Or you might be starting out in your career, and do not have a current employer. Perhaps everyone in your company posts their resumes online.

For clients of mine who are *not* at risk of causing waves with a current employer, I always recommend that they consider posting a resume. It is one of the best ways to signal to us recruiters that you're open to being contacted.

You can post your resume for just a day or two if you'd like to see how it goes. Or you can post it for the entire time that you are job seeking. You can even keep your resume posted permanently, updating it every time that you enter a new role.

I see all types and approaches in my work; there are no rules about this. The choice is yours.

A Few Caveats for Resume Posting

Let's say that you do decide to post your resume online. Here are a few scenarios I'd like you to be prepared for:

1. You may be contacted about job openings that aren't a great fit. This is very common, and to be expected.
2. You may be contacted by people who promise to find you a job in exchange for money. This isn't common, but it does happen on occasion.
3. Your contact information might be "harvested" by companies that are collecting data. I'm not sure how common this is, but read on for a method of protecting against that possibility.

The first challenge—being pitched on jobs that aren't a fit—is something that you should expect. Many recruiters are working at a breakneck pace, and often don't understand the nuances of the roles they're trying to fill.

This is especially true for highly technical positions. Recruiters may pitch positions to you that are outside your scope of knowledge or interest. If you have a few minutes, you can explain to them precisely what you do, and why this role isn't a fit. Or you can simply choose not to respond. We recruiters are used to that!

To smooth out communication and save time, I encourage you to state, right at the top of your posted resume, any preferences or parameters.

For example:

> "Recruiters: I am only interested in work-from-home remote opportunities."

> "I am only interested in part-time (20 hour/week maximum) roles."

> "I am interested in IT management roles, not software development."

> "I am willing to relocate only to Los Angeles. I am not open to relocate to any other location."

Or whatever else you'd like to say. We welcome these points of clarification. These statements probably shouldn't appear on a resume that you send in for a job application. However, for posted resumes, they are perfectly appropriate and welcome.

The second challenge—people approaching you for money—is to be avoided. If someone promises you that they'll get you a job if you pay them, it's likely a scam.

Recruiters like me are paid by the companies we work for, *not* by you. Legitimate recruiters *never* charge candidates. Not ever. If someone encourages you to give them money in order to get a job, I'd recommend ceasing all communication. It's very likely a scam.

The third challenge—having your contact information gathered—can be mitigated. Here is what I recommend to my clients who decide to post their resumes online:

Create a new Gmail email address for your job search, and only use that Gmail account on your resume. Do not use your personal email address.

Sign up for a Google Voice phone number connected to that Gmail email address, and only include that on your resume. Do not use your own phone number.

Include your city/state/zip (as many of us recruiters will be searching resumes geographically), but do not include your street address.

You can then set your new Gmail email address and Google Voice number to forward to your primary email and phone number. You can turn off this forwarding whenever you'd like.

That way, you're buffered from unwanted emails and calls. Your personal contact information is also protected. You can turn off the flow of communication whenever you want.

So to recap: The primary risk of posting your resume is that your current employer may see the resume. Also, you will probably be approached for jobs that aren't a great fit. Some people might try to get you to pay them to find you work. Your contact information might be harvested. That last issue can be mitigated by using a new email and phone number, and leaving out your street address.

Now for the big benefit. By posting your resume, you are sending a signal to us recruiters that you'd like to be contacted. This puts you at the very top of our lists for many roles. We prefer not to bother people who are uninterested in new opportunities.

However, we rarely know who is and who isn't open. By posting your resume, you are moving yourself to the top of our lists.

As an example of this, let's say that I am working on a search for a Sales Manager for a lasers company. I will likely spend weeks cold-calling sales executives at lasers companies, networking with people in the lasers industry, researching, chatting, and cold-calling some more. This will take a great deal of work.

However, before I do any of that, I'll run a quick search on various resume databases—including those at specialty job sites dedicated to lasers. Why not start with people who are open to being contacted? Those people will pop to the top of my list.

You, too, can pop to the top of lists by making your resume available online. Again, please do not post your resume if you are at risk of harmful ripple-effects from your current employer. But if that isn't a concern, resume posting is a great way to open the door to opportunities.

LinkedIn

The other way to make yourself visible to recruiters is to create a profile on LinkedIn, and become as connected as possible.

Most of us recruiters use LinkedIn on a daily basis. The most basic subscription level gives us visibility to our immediate group of connections, plus anyone connected to our connections, plus anyone connected to those people. So there's a "three level deep" group of people whom we can see and contact. In order to expand past that, we need to pay for higher subscription levels.

I share this because many recruiters at small companies will only be able to see your profile if you're in their first three tiers. In order to reach that level of visibility, I recommend connecting with at least a hundred people.

Once you have a hundred or so connections, you'll start to become quite visible to many recruiters. Don't worry about making thousands of connections (although that certainly can help!)

Who can these connections be? Anyone at all. Friends, family members, high school or college classmates, current or past coworkers. They can be people on your softball team, folks you volunteer with, or your neighbors. LinkedIn asks that you have some connection with these people, so it's best not to send invites to strangers. (Although many recruiters will be happy to receive unsolicited connection requests.)

LinkedIn also allows you to signal that you are "open to work." This is similar to posting a resume.

As of this writing, there are two levels of visibility about your openness to work. You can:

1. indicate *only* to recruiters that you're open to work, rather than the general public; or
2. indicate it to everyone, with a special flair on your photo.

The risks and benefits I covered in the resume section apply here as well. Your current employer might see that you've tagged yourself as open to work, and this can lead to ripple-effects. However, many recruiters will also see you, and might approach you with job opportunities.

What to Include

When you're creating your LinkedIn profile, it's important to include as many relevant keywords as possible.

Many people simply list their company and title on their profile. While that is OK, you will be *much* more visible if you include keyword-rich descriptions of the work you've done. These keywords are what we recruiters are frequently searching on.

As an example, I'm currently working on a search for an Embedded Systems Electrical Engineer. I am searching on keywords like "FPGA" (field programmable gate array) and "Zynq" (a specific brand of chip).

People who have included those keywords in their profiles pop up in my search results. People who haven't included those aren't as visible.

As part of your keyword mix, you can include acronyms—and *also* write out what the acronyms stand for. We recruiters may be searching on either the acronym or the phrase, so it's a good idea to include both.

For example, restaurant managers might say "back of house (BOH)." Medical workers might say, "electronic health record (EHR) system." Or for a cleaner look, you can simply alternate the acronym and the phrase throughout your profile.

It's also helpful to include specific systems, software, and other products that you use in your work: point-of-sale systems, electronic record systems, software platforms. We recruiters might be searching on specific names, brands, or manufacturers like the Zynq chip I mentioned above.

One easy way to add keywords to your LinkedIn profile is to update the "skills and endorsements" section. As of this writing, you can add 50 skills to your profile. These skills become searchable keywords as soon as you add them.

LinkedIn will not try to confirm how skilled you actually are at any of these. Please add any skills that you consider applicable!

What Not to Include

What you *shouldn't* include is anything that is confidential information. I have seen people list private company sales figures on their LinkedIn profiles—information that is not meant for public knowledge. Displaying this may cause a new company concern.

Please also don't include anything that is an attack on a past employer. I have seen profiles that accused companies of fraud, mismanagement, and other acts of malfeasance. If you feel the need to post comments about past employers, it's best to limit these comments to employee review sites like Glassdoor, where you can post anonymously.

Finally (and this is just common sense), please don't include anything mocking or exclusionary in your LinkedIn profile. I have seen dozens of profiles that were filled with sarcastic, demeaning statements—often directed toward politicians, but sometimes directed toward people of a particular nationality, orientation, or other group.

If you have this type of material on LinkedIn, I recommend that you remove it. It may have been intended as humor. However, it is visible to those of us in recruiting and will cause most employers concern. Even if you've "liked" someone else's posting of this sort, the post will show up in your activity feed.

I ask my clients to take a close look at their profiles, and try to imagine how an HR person might view the content. I encourage everyone to remove postings that express intolerance—even if these postings were meant to be sarcastically humorous.

Companies are filled with people who hold a diversity of values, beliefs, orientations, and creeds. Almost every company wants to maintain a professional, welcoming environment. Hostile, sarcastic posts will trigger concern in almost every human resources professional. It's best to eliminate anything of that sort.

Open Communication

Let me make one last suggestion before I move on to the next section. I encourage you to dialogue with recruiters who reach out to you, even if you're not interested in their immediate opening.

Let me give an example of how this can be helpful. Let's say that I contact someone in Texas about a position in Boston.

The person says to me, "Dan, I want to stay in Texas. But if you have something in the Dallas or Austin area—or something that can be done remotely—I'd be interested."

That's great information for me. Perhaps a few weeks later, my corporate client lets me know that the position I'm working on is now remote-eligible. I can now reach back to that person in Texas and see if she might be interested.

Her willingness to tell me her preferences opened the door for opportunities. And of course, perhaps I'll start working with a client in Texas someday! If so, she's on my list of people to call.

Letting recruiters know your preferences can lead to future fits. It's great to form those relationships and keep the communication flowing.

Third Avenue:
Conversations

Applying for job ads and becoming visible to recruiters were the first two job search methods we covered. Now let's move on to the most common way that people find jobs: *conversations*.

This third avenue is the big one. As I mentioned, as many as 80% of jobs are found through personal and professional connections.

I am not going to use the word "networking" to describe this approach. Networking, for many people, has a connotation of "using" people to "get" something (in this case, a job).

Many of my clients have said to me, "Dan, I hate networking. I refuse to do it. I refuse to use people and have ulterior motives and agendas like that."

In response to that concern, let me introduce a concept that I call "flipping the script." If there is just one thing that you take from this book, I would like it to be this concept. I will return to this throughout the chapters to come as well.

Here's what I mean by flipping the script:

Most people approach the job search process with the attitude of, "I need to get a job." This is completely normal. There's nothing wrong with that approach.

However, in order to be more successful, I propose that you flip the script in your job search, and approach the process with an attitude of, "Here's what I'm excited to *give*."

Instead of focusing on what you want to get (a job), you can lead with all that you have to give (your talents, abilities, and other gifts.) This can change the entire process of job-searching in powerful ways. It brings a whole new tone to the endeavor.

Let me give a personal example of this to illustrate what I mean.

A few weeks after I graduated from my counseling program, I set up a therapy practice. Instead of focusing on *getting* clients, I instead focused on how I could *give* to them.

I asked myself: How can I give most fully to people that want therapy help?

The first thing that came to mind was to offer my services on a sliding-scale. That seemed like a good way to help people who might be struggling financially.

Next, I created a website with worksheets and therapy tools. I was happy to give information to people, regardless of whether or not they came to me for sessions.

I rented offices in two different cities, 45 minutes apart. This ensured that people wouldn't have to travel very far to see me. I also created session openings in the evenings, in order to make it easy for people with daytime jobs.

When I met people at coffee shops or elsewhere, I handed out my business card and said, "In case you know of anyone who is struggling with career or other issues, I'm happy to help."

Within 12 weeks of doing this, my practice was completely full. I began to run a waiting list, and soon there were people on my waiting list three months out. At that point, I stopped the waiting list and began to refer everyone to other therapists.

For the next decade, my practice remained completely full. By focusing 100% on what I could give to potential clients, I ended up with far more clients than I could handle.

I share this story because conversations connected to your job search don't have to be focused on getting a job, or getting a lead, or getting anything else. Instead, your conversations can be focused on all that you have to *give*.

When you meet someone, you can describe to them the gifts you're eager to share, and the help you're excited to offer. This will be far more impactful—and enjoyable—than the conventional networking approach.

An Example of Flipping the Script

As an example of this flip to giving, let's say that you're at your weekly softball club. The old-fashioned way to "network" might look like this:

"Hey," your friend says. "How are you?"

"OK, I guess," you say. "I'm actually looking for a job. If you hear of an opening for a Medical Assistant, let me know."

"Medical Assistant? OK, got it. That's not really my field, but I'll let you know if I see anything."

"Great, thanks."

"No problem. Good luck."

Now, that's probably not going to produce any results. That's the old approach—"I'm trying to get a job. Let me know if you hear of anything." There's nothing wrong with that method, though it's unlikely to produce a large number of leads.

Here's how the new, giving-focused approach might look:

"Hey," your friend says. "How are you?"

"Doing fine," you say. "I'm actually at a point where I'm looking for a busy medical office to help. I love working with patients and helping doctors. I'm excited to find a medical office that needs some extra hands. The busier the better."

"That's great," says your friend. "You know, come to think of it, my doctor's office was slammed the other day. I had to wait 45 minutes to get into my appointment. Let me know if you want the

THE JOB SEARCH

name of the place."

That was a small shift, but you can see the difference. In the first approach, you told your friend that you were looking for a Medical Assistant job. He'll keep his eyes open for you, but that's about it.

In the second approach, you described what you enjoy and how eager you are to help. That immediately triggered a memory of your friend having to wait at his doctor's office. You didn't mention a job, a title, or any details of your job search. You simply led with your *enthusiasm to help.*

Is your friend's doctor currently advertising a job for a Medical Assistant? Who knows! Your friend certainly doesn't know. But he does know a busy medical practice that perhaps could use some help. He just gave you a good initial lead.

Here are some other examples of "giving" statements:

"I'm a designer, and love to help companies develop everything from websites to brochures. I enjoy helping people to get messages out."

"Kids are so much fun. I'm always excited to connect with families that need help with babysitting."

"Flying is my greatest joy. I really love being a pilot. I'm excited to find new opportunities to fly."

If someone said that last statement to me, it would get my wheels turning.

I might say, "I hear the local flight schools flying over my house from time to time. Have you talked to them? And now that I think about it, a friend's brother-in-law flies for UPS. I think they're about to hire some people. And I once met a glider launch pilot here in town. I wonder if that company needs people?"

If instead the person said, "I'm looking for a job as a pilot. Let me know if you hear of any openings," I'd probably just say, "Sorry, haven't heard of anything."

The point is that by focusing on what you want to give, and expressing your eagerness to share your gifts, you are much more likely to open avenues.

Flipping the Script in Networking Meetings

Let me now take this a notch deeper, and discuss conversations in a more "classic networking" setting.

Imagine that you're seeking a new job as a hotel manager. A mutual acquaintance introduces you to the owner of a hotel, who is willing to have a chat with you.

In your conversation with the hotel owner, the old-fashioned approach would be to say, "I'm looking for a job as a hotel manager. Please let me know if you have an opening, or hear of one."

There's nothing wrong with that approach. It's how networking has been done for decades. It's a perfectly acceptable way to go about things.

However, a far more impactful strategy might be to say something like this:

"Thank you for chatting with me, Ms. Jones. Aren't we lucky to be in hospitality? I've really been enjoying the increase in tourism traffic. At this point in my life, I'm really excited to help a hotel that values its customers, and treats each visit as precious. I enjoy giving visitors five-star treatment, and am looking forward to finding a place that can use help with that."

Ms. Jones is smart; she gets that you're looking for new opportunities. But you're leading the conversation not by asking for a job or leads, but by expressing your enthusiasm and ways that you like to be of help.

There is no explicit "ask" of Ms. Jones. There is nothing you're trying to get from her. You're simply expressing your enthusiasm for hotel management, your values, and your desire to give your gifts.

As you say this, you're allowing Ms. Jones to respond in whatever way she wants—which is itself a gift. There is no pressure whatsoever on her. (The sense of pressure to "get" job leads is what usually leads people to hate conventional networking.)

If you want to put icing on the cake, you can flip the script completely and ask Ms. Jones if there's anything you can do to help *her*!

You might, for example, say, "Ms. Jones, please let me know if there's anything your hotel is struggling with. If I can be of help myself, great. If not, I might know of someone in the industry that could assist you. I'm always happy to make connections."

Instead of trying to get something from her in this conversation, you're entirely focused on giving. I myself end many business-oriented conversations by asking the person if there's anything that they can use help with. Very few people are asked that question, and most people are touched by the offer.

Reflexive Empathy

Let me conclude this chapter by sharing a psychological concept that builds on this.

In the world of psychology, there's a dynamic called *reflexive empathy* where one person's mind "mirrors" another person's.

We've all seen this in conflict situations: One person's anger triggers another person's anger, and a cycle of escalation forms.

This same dynamic can be used in positive ways. In the example above, your spirit of enthusiasm and helpfulness will very likely trigger *Ms. Jones's* spirit of enthusiasm and helpfulness.

Her mind will very likely mirror yours, to some degree. An alignment will take place.

Even if Ms. Jones doesn't have an opening at her own hotel, she might suddenly recall a fellow hotel owner who is losing a manager to retirement. Her desire to be helpful—sparked by *your* desire to be helpful—might bring that, or other leads, to her mind.

I encourage you to experiment with this in your day-to-day conversations. Try leading with a spirit of enthusiastic helpfulness, and note if the people you're talking to enter into a similar mindset themselves. You may find that this happens frequently, especially when you're talking with sensitive and empathetic people.

I will be discussing this giving dynamic in the chapters to come. For now, let me dive deeper into the process of job searching with a series of Q&A's.

CHAPTER FIVE

The Job Search: A Deeper Look

As a reminder, there are three primary methods of finding new jobs:

1. You can apply for jobs that are advertised.
2. You can make yourself visible so that recruiters like me can find you.
3. You can have conversations about what you are excited to give through your work.

The following are some questions I have been asked about the job search process.

Q: I have zero excitement for job searching. I would be faking it if I tried to come across as enthusiastic. Are you saying that I should lie about how I feel?

A: Certainly not. I'm very sympathetic about how exhausting, overwhelming, stressful, and at times discouraging the job search process can be. That is one of the reasons that I wrote this book.

However, the fact remains that people will tend to align with your state of mind. If you come across as unenthusiastic in your job search, the people you interact with may respond in much the same way.

So what can you do about this? One technique is to choose some small (perhaps some *tiny*) part of your work that you are enthusiastic about, and allow your mind to focus on that one part. Let that little spark guide your search.

To illustrate this, let me return to my early jobs that I described at the beginning of this book. All of those jobs were fairly miserable experiences, at least to me at the time. However, there were aspects of each that I could describe enthusiastically.

At the computer store, I was exposed to new video games as soon as they were released. At the road-paving job, I got to drive a big truck around town. At my urban planning job, I worked for a boss who was kind and compassionate. At the detergent company, I developed a customer demo with technology called "HyperCard"—a precursor to internet websites, which would later form the basis for a new branch in my career.

There were aspects of each job that I found interesting.

In a similar way, there are probably at least a few elements of your work that you're enthusiastic about. I recommend that you focus on those as you're conducting your job search. Allow those aspects to remain front and center.

This isn't just an emotional trick. As you focus on parts of your work that you enjoy, you will gravitate toward opportunities that include those elements.

Let's say, for example, that you're currently working as a clerk in a construction permit office. You enjoy the interactions with the public. However, you dislike many other elements of the work: the layers of bureaucracy, the slow speed, the culture of the office.

When you describe your work to people, you can focus on how much you enjoy interacting with the public and helping them with needs. You can ignore the rest of your work experience, and allow your enthusiasm for helping people to shine away all else.

Someone you talk to might suggest an opening that has nothing to do with clerking or permitting, but does involve helping

THE JOB SEARCH Q&A

the public. Let that bright spot in your work life guide your path forward. Release your focus on all the other aspects as you talk to people about what you enjoy.

Again, I do want to acknowledge how emotionally draining job searching can be. It is completely normal to feel frustrated, discouraged, or anything else.

And yet—if you can find a spark of enthusiasm, allow it to grow, and approach your job search with its light, you will likely navigate the process with far more ease.

Q: Is it OK to contact an employee at a company I like, and let them know that I want to work for their company?

A: Let me give a nuanced answer for this one.

First, it's fine in almost all cases to contact people in human resources—recruiters, HR managers, and so forth. The mission for those of us in human resources is to recruit and retain employees. We're happy to hear from job seekers interested in working with us.

Many companies will have a careers@ or jobs@ address on their website that goes right to the HR staff. You are welcome to send a cover letter and unsolicited resume directly to that email. Simply explain who you are and what you are seeking. If a company doesn't have a current job opening that is a match, they will probably be happy to hold onto your information for the future.

What usually *doesn't* go well is to randomly contact employees and say, "Please help me get a job with your company."

I know folks who are irritated—even offended—by these types of messages. "I'm not in HR, and I don't know this person," they say. "Why would I drop what I'm doing to help this person find a job?"

Between those two options there is plenty of middle-ground. You can, for example, reach out to someone in a company, politely introduce yourself, and ask for the contact information of the company recruiter or HR manager. Most people will be fine with this. Some may even take you under their wing and help you with the process.

You can also look to see if you have "friends of friends" on LinkedIn or Facebook who work at your target companies. If so, you can ask your friend if they would be willing to introduce you to the employee. This is softer than a cold-call.

Now, I do want to acknowledge that many people have landed jobs by being daring and contacting executives at companies directly. It's certainly a valid approach. I have even heard of people who took creative approaches like "tweeting" their interest in jobs at a company's Twitter account.

So the approach is up to you. I personally would not recommend calling employees at random; you don't want to make a poor impression by annoying people who are not involved with hiring. It's best to talk to a recruiter, an HR manager, or perhaps (as long as you're polite and not pushy) the person who you'd actually be working for.

One exception to this: In retail and other non-corporate environments, it's usually fine to ask employees how to apply for work. Retail sales associates, restaurant workers, people in skilled and unskilled trades, and folks in the hospitality industry generally receive a large number of these "walk in" inquiries. Most will be happy to point you in the right direction.

Q: You talked about spending 5 to 15 minutes a day looking at job ads. But I am out of work, and have time on my hands. What should I spend the rest of my time doing?

A: You're of course free to spend as much time looking at job ads as you'd like. However, I find that most people reach a fatigue point rather quickly. A strategy of small, daily steps is often better than taking a few big, infrequent leaps.

Having said that, perhaps you find it enjoyable to look through job ads and send in resumes. If so, spend as much time as you wish! Experiment with whatever schedule feels sustainable to you on a day-to-day basis.

Regardless of how much time you spend looking through job ads, there are many other helpful things you can do with your day. You can go to a coffee shop and chat with the folks there. You can volunteer at a charity. You can join book groups, hiking groups, sports groups, or anything else.

You can offer to help any friends who run businesses. You can offer your own services on a freelance basis. You can sign up for a class or training. (Check your local state "workforce" or employment center for free classes they might offer.)

While you're doing all of these things, let people know how excited you are to offer your gifts. Ask them if you can be of help to them in any way. These conversations are very likely to point you in a direction of a new opportunity.

What you *shouldn't* do is sit alone at home feeling frustrated or guilty that you can't find a job. That is perhaps the worst way to spend your day. Instead, get active, be helpful, and let people know how eager you are to share your gifts. You might be surprised at how things unfold from there.

Q: I'm not shy about bothering people. I was planning to blast out to everyone I know that I'm looking for a new job. Is that OK?

A: Certainly! If you are comfortable letting people know about your job search, by all means—blast away. Let your friends, neighbors, former co-workers, industry contacts, professors, and any strangers you meet know what you're seeking. You can also contact people in your industry to introduce yourself.

To be most successful, it's best to approach the process with an enthusiastic-yet-humble stance. Sometimes a "blast" approach can come across as overly pushy, and it's best to minimize that. Note how people are responding to you. Are they excited to help you? Do they brainstorm with you, and offer creative ideas? If so, you're on a good track.

If you can combine a friendly, humble tone with an energetic, communicative approach, you will probably find many new job opportunities very quickly.

You'll also have a great career in sales, if you choose to go down that road!

Q: I'm very shy and hate to bother people. It is very difficult for me to talk about myself. I'm not sure if I can use any of the outreach techniques you're talking about. Do you have any suggestions?

A: First of all, you're in good company. Almost half of people consider themselves shy. Even many non-shy folks don't feel comfortable talking to people about their search for employment.

My suggestion is to use the approach I described in the last chapter: Set aside a few minutes each day and take one small, manageable step. You get to choose what this is. It should be something that feels like a "stretch" but not overwhelming or painful.

Then, the next day, take another small step. Then another the next day. You might find that by the end of a week or two, you've developed more comfort with the outreach process.

What might these steps be?

Well, let's say that you are very close to your sister. Perhaps you can write her an email and let her know that you're starting a job search. That's it for the day.

If she writes back asking questions, then you can share a little more detail with her the next day.

The day after that, you can let a friend know that you're looking for work.

THE JOB SEARCH Q&A

The following day, you can sign up for a Gmail and Google Voice account, and consider posting your resume with those contact elements.

And so on. The key is to take many manageable steps, one day at a time. Please do not overwhelm yourself. The goal here is to develop a sense of comfort and ease with the process. The best way to develop that ease is with a series of small, incremental moves.

Also, please keep in mind that you're not really bothering anyone. You're simply letting people know that you're available to help with your skills, abilities, and gifts. This is a wonderful thing.

If the people you reach out to happen to have an idea or suggestion, great! If not, you haven't troubled them at all by sharing a brief email, message, or text.

Q: *I have a real problem applying for jobs that I'm not excited about. Why are you encouraging us to apply for things that are "in the ballpark"? Why shouldn't I hold out for something I'm truly excited about?*

A: As I say to my clients, the pace of your job search is completely up to you.

If you feel comfortable being selective and waiting until you find jobs that you're highly excited about, that's fine.

However, I have found that many people fall into a pattern of looking through job ads for weeks until they finally find one that interests them. They apply for that job, wait a month, and become disappointed when they don't hear back. After that it's another set of weeks or months before applying for another position. Years can pass like this.

By applying for "in the ballpark" jobs on a regular basis, you keep a momentum going. If you're invited to interview for a job and decide that you're not interested, you can always decline the interview. Simply let the company know that you're pursuing another opportunity.

If you do agree to an interview and are offered a position, you can choose to turn it down. There's no requirement to accept a job offer—or even to take additional steps at any phase of the process.

Having said that, you might find that once you meet with a company about an "in the ballpark" job, your view of the job changes. Perhaps you and your potential supervisor hit it off, and the job begins to seem very attractive. Perhaps the manager is willing to modify the role to fit your skills more fully. Or perhaps your personality clashes with hers, and you have no interest in proceeding. You'll never know unless you apply.

There is, of course, an obvious reason that most of us don't want to apply for numerous jobs: We don't want to swing and miss over and over. That experience can feel deflating. I respect your choice and comfort about this.

However, let me share that one of my favorite things about my own career is that I get to face "failure" every day.

I have contacted thousands of people for a single job opening without filling it. I have reached out to hundreds of companies at times without finding clients. I have swung and missed on pitches to business owners, to candidates, and even to assistants I contacted for help. I am thankful for these experiences, as they taught me to roll with the process.

I believe that there really aren't "rejections" and "failures" in a job search. There are simply attempts to form relationships that—at least for now—didn't blossom. That doesn't mean that anyone is rejected, failed, or did anything wrong. It simply means that the click didn't happen at this time, in this form.

I encourage you to look at things in that way. You are offering to help a company. If they don't take you up on your offer at this time, they may do so in the future. Your application for their opening is a gift.

Offer your help freely, and then move on to offer help to someone else.

Q: *I'm starting out in a new field. However, I'm not sure how to find jobs that will let me start from scratch. I search for "entry level," but I don't see much. Do you have any suggestions?*

A: Sure. Searching for keywords like "entry level" (and also "entry-level" with the hyphen) is a good start.

You can also search on keywords like "junior," "graduates," (even if you're not a recent graduate), "training," "no experience," and similar terms. On many job posting sites, you can set a filter for jobs tagged as entry level, or requiring 0-3 years of experience.

Let me offer a number of additional approaches to consider as well.

First, if you have worked in another field and you're switching into something new, you may be qualified for non-entry roles. You may have plenty of transferable skills. I encourage you to go ahead and apply for jobs that require some experience. Simply explain, in a cover letter, how your existing experience crosses over to this role.

If you are new to the world of work, you can look through job ads posted at your high school, college, or alumni career site. It's often OK to use these career services even if you're several years out of school. Almost all of the jobs posted in these forums will be geared toward entry-level applicants.

Internships are another avenue for entry-level job seekers. Both of my Manhattan jobs were internships, which paid the equivalent of minimum wage. Apprenticeship programs in the skilled trades are similar to internships, and are geared toward entry-level folks.

Career fairs are a bit old school, but they're still used. At career fairs, employers set up booths and pitch their openings to attendees. Many of these will be entry-level or have a low experience requirement.

Staffing and temp agencies are often happy to be approached by entry-level job seekers. Some agencies specialize in office jobs, some in manufacturing or technical jobs, and others in medical fields. A temp job can be a great way to get your foot in the door with a company or industry.

State-run employment centers—often called "workforce centers" or "career centers"—are open to the public, and offer a variety of employment assistance. You might be able to access free resume writing assistance and other career counseling services at these centers.

Please also use the other approaches I've covered in this book. Apply for any interesting opportunities that seem like they're in the ballpark—even if you don't have the experience required. It's quite possible that the company wrote an "ideal wish list" job description and are flexible about actual requirements. They may soften their needs as they interview candidates.

Consider posting your resume online, both on general and specialty sites (for example, sites for veterans if you've served in the military). Create a robust LinkedIn profile, connect with people you know, and mark your profile as "open to work." Have real-world conversations with as many people as you feel comfortable with—and let them know how enthusiastic you are about what you want to give.

Feel free to reach out to companies and express your interest in working for them. This could involve talking with a store worker or manager, as I did with my first job. Or you could simply email the careers@ or jobs@ email address on a company website with a resume and cover letter.

Many companies don't advertise their entry-level positions because they regularly receive inquiries from entry-level job seekers. You can be one of those people. Contacting a company proactively shows initiative.

Almost all of us HR professionals are happy to receive email introductions from entry-level job seekers. After all, we never know when we will have additional needs.

Q: Are there ways to reduce the sense of being overwhelmed in a job search that you described?

A: Sure, let me share an approach that I use in my therapy practice. This can be used in the context of job searches, as well as in other areas that are causing you stress.

I frequently draw what I call the "TEA Cycle" on a whiteboard in my counseling sessions. TEA stands for Thoughts, Emotions, and Actions. All three of these aspects tend to work in concert, creating a spiral effect.

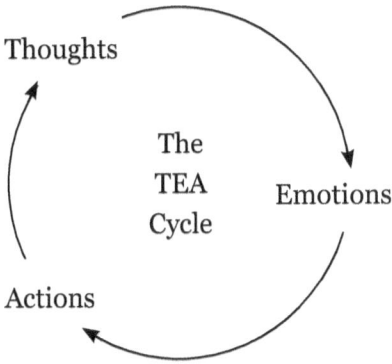

If you're like many people, you may be having thoughts during your job search that go like this:

<u>Thoughts</u>
"I have to find a job!"
"But I'm not seeing anything good."
"Maybe I'll never find anything that's a fit."
"But I have to find something soon!"

And so on. These thoughts will give rise to various emotions. For example:

<u>Emotions</u>
A sense of pressure
Disappointment
Worry
More pressure

Quite the difficult cocktail of emotions!

Both of those facets—thoughts and emotions—will influence the third aspect, actions.

Many people fall into a job search action pattern like this:

<u>Actions</u>
Procrastinate
Procrastinate some more
Slam into high gear for a while
Procrastinate again

Your TEA Cycle might be different, of course. Everyone is unique. But I have seen cycles like the above many times.

Let me suggest a way to work with each of these elements.

For the *thoughts* part of the TEA Cycle, you can develop a new set of de-pressuring thoughts. You can strengthen these new thoughts by writing them down on a piece of paper and placing the paper where you will see it regularly.

The new de-pressuring thoughts can be ones like:

"It's OK to do this job search in small steps."
"Five minutes each day is enough."
"It can't hurt to apply for a job, even if it's not a perfect fit."
"It's fine to send in an application that feels like a stretch."

The goal is to choose new thoughts that remove a sense of pressure, hopelessness, worry, or whatever else was overwhelming you. This "thought swapping" practice is the basis of cognitive therapy. It can be very powerful.

You may need to plug in the new thoughts repeatedly before they begin to stick around. That is why I recommend writing one or two on a piece of paper, and reviewing the thoughts as much as you can throughout the day. You will be forming a new habit as you do this.

Let's move on to the *emotions* part of the cycle. You might find "mindfulness" approaches to be helpful at this stage. Mindfulness involves present-moment awareness.

As an emotional mindfulness practice, take a few seconds and allow yourself to fully experience your current emotions—even if they're uncomfortable emotions like anxiety or a sense of pressure.

Allow those emotions to be fully in your awareness, without resistance. Touch into them for a moment. Note how they feel. Allow them to be present without fighting them.

Then give them permission to flow through and past your awareness. Invite a clean new experience of the next moment to arise.

Emotions tend to come and go—especially if we don't fight, feed, or flee from them. Allow each new moment to replace the last, without resistance.

As you do this, you might find that a new emotion arises. Then the old one might pop back; then the new one returns. As you allow your feelings to simply arise and pass through your awareness, you may begin to sense a place of calm just behind them all. Allow yourself to rest in that peaceful place if you are able.

There are many other ways to work with emotions. Some people use exercise to direct the energy of the emotion. This is a very common technique in behavioral therapy. Other people channel emotions into creative outlets like journaling, painting, singing, or dance.

For the *actions* stage, I always recommend replacing a pattern of "procrastinate, procrastinate, slam into high gear, procrastinate," with small, easy, manageable daily steps forward. I have covered this in several places throughout this book.

Instead of oscillating between procrastination and intense effort, you can simply focus on taking one or two small steps each day.

Does this small-steps approach require patience? Yes, it does. Does it require persistence? Yes, that too. But it is a far better action pattern, in my opinion, than the procrastinate-and-slam cycle that many people fall into.

Self-care actions are also helpful actions. Buy yourself a treat to enjoy while you're doing your job search steps. Bring your computer to a favorite coffee shop and do your steps there. Ask a friend to be with you as you do your steps. Combine the job search steps with a reward of your choosing.

The goal is to form a new, energy-increasing TEA Cycle to replace the old, energy-draining one that was in place before. Feel free to experiment with changes to all three phases, and see what works for you.

•

Let me conclude this chapter by summarizing the themes I have covered about searching for jobs.

There are three main avenues for seeking job opportunities:

1. You can apply for jobs that are posted.
2. You can become visible so that recruiters can find you.
3. You can have conversations with people about offering your gifts.

THE JOB SEARCH Q&A

For the job-posting approach, you may want to bookmark a variety of job sites: (1) general sites like Indeed, LinkedIn, and Monster; (2) specialty sites for different fields or groups; (3) company websites; and (4) websites of government entities.

If you're trying to enter a new field, you can consider applying for apprenticeship programs and internships. You can visit job fairs or employment centers (often known as workforce centers.) Staffing and employment agencies may also be of help.

In order to become more visible to recruiters, you can post your resume online—for example, on Indeed or Monster. I *only* recommend this if there is no risk of creating ripple-effects with your current employer. I encourage you to use a new email and phone number on your resume if you do choose to post it.

You can also build a robust LinkedIn profile with connections and keywords, and mark that you are "open to work" (but again, only if broadcasting that doesn't put you at risk with your current employer.)

The conversations approach is the most powerful. You can chat with HR managers, recruiters, hiring managers, and friends-of-friends at companies you're interested in. As I mentioned, it's perfectly acceptable to "cold approach" an HR person. Many employees will be happy to point the way toward their company recruiters and HR staff if you introduce yourself and ask politely.

You can also have conversations with people in your social network—family, friends, neighbors, classmates, or anyone else. If traditional "networking" approaches don't appeal to you, you can instead lead the conversations by simply sharing how you would like to use your gifts.

You don't need to ask anyone for anything, if you don't feel comfortable doing so. You can simply let people know how enthusiastic you are to use your abilities. Your enthusiasm will very likely trigger theirs, and they might have some ideas for you.

Job searching can be exhausting. Therefore, I recommend that you take it in small, daily steps. I also recommend that you reinforce some de-pressuring thoughts while you do your work, and use mindfulness practices to allow emotions to pass by like clouds in the sky.

Learning to job search in a peaceful way is a remarkable accomplishment. Any steps you can take toward that goal are worth the effort.

Let me now move on to the next step in the process: writing a resume and cover letter, and filling out an application.

CHAPTER SIX

Resumes, Cover Letters, and Applications

Finally we come to everyone's favorite career subject: resumes!

Just kidding; most people dislike resumes. Even many career counselors avoid working on them.

I am a bit unusual, in that I've always had a curious affinity for the things. Even back in college, I was the guy who gave out resume tips to anyone who would listen.

All these years later, I spend much of my day reading through resumes. I've probably reviewed over a quarter-million of them during the course of my career. I've had job postings which received a thousand resumes in a week, and I've spent a chunk of my work life searching through resume databases.

I've also helped many of my career counseling clients write resumes. I don't do the writing for my clients; we work together, and they do most of the writing themselves. But I do help my clients understand how companies are viewing what they write.

In this chapter, I'll discuss resumes from the perspective of a recruiter. I will show you what we look for, how quickly we read each section, and what elements are most important. I will also discuss how to write a simple, clear cover letter.

Resumes: The Basics

Before I begin, let me state that articles about "how to write a resume" usually make me frown.

I tend to agree with 80% of the suggestions in these articles. But other 20% of tips seem completely off-base.

Suggestions like, "Use an unusual format to stand out from the crowd," or "Include colorful graphics on your resume," are simply not wise. Those resume tips aren't written by people who have to read through piles of these things.

When you're crafting your resume, think of us recruiters and have pity! We are generally working under enormous time pressure, and may have hundreds of resumes to process each day.

Because of that, the best practice is keep your resume *clear, simple, and customized to the job at hand*. We recruiters would love to find a match between your skills and our jobs. We are searching all day for matches, often frantically. If we have to spend time navigating unusual resume layouts or formats, we will probably give in to fatigue and move on.

In this chapter, I'll share many ways to make your resume, cover letter, and application pop. But that will only happen if the overall package is readable.

Keeping your resume clear and easy to process is the most important thing you can do. Although that's not very sexy advice (and it wouldn't make for an exciting "resume tips" article), it's the truth.

Resume Length

Let me begin the discussion of resumes by answering a common question: How long should your resume be?

My answer is: Your resume should be as concise as you can make it, while still including as much relevant information as possible.

Practically speaking, I generally recommend that:

People who are *early* in their careers should have one-page resumes.

People who are in the *middle* of their careers should have two-page resumes.

People in *senior* positions can have three-page resumes.

No one should have more than three pages.

Now, there are a few exceptions. Folks in academia often have a "Curriculum Vitae" (CV) which contain lists of published research papers, patents, and so forth. If you're applying for an academic position, a lengthy CV is appropriate and expected.

On the opposite side of things, an attorney friend of mine told me that one-page resumes are expected for all law applicants at his company, regardless of seniority level. I've never recruited in the legal field, so I defer to him. There may be other fields where single-page resumes are the norm even for experienced people.

For general purposes, though, I like the lengths above. One page for junior folks. Two pages for most people. Three pages for very experienced people. No one outside of academia needs a four (or ten) page resume.

These are not simply my own preferences. I've had corporate clients say to me, "Dan, why does this person need five pages to describe his work history? If he can't communicate concisely, he's not a fit." I've had to battle to give these candidates a chance for an interview. Their overly long resumes made it harder for me to advocate for them.

You can safely assume that everyone who reads your resume is busy, tired, and eager to get to the end of the recruiting process as quickly as possible. No one will be looking for a good, long read. Resumes that *very quickly* show matches between your skills and the job you're applying for are the best.

Having said that, let me share a few caveats.

First, don't cram things in order to hit the page lengths I mentioned. Don't run text close to the edges or eliminate spacing between lines. The layout of your resume should appear as normal as possible, with at least half-inch margins on all sides. It's better to edit-down content than to squash it all in.

Also, it's not a good idea to use very small fonts, as some readers of your resume may have less-than-perfect eyesight. If your readers struggle to process the content of your resume, they will be tempted to move on to another candidate. I encourage you to bump up small fonts by a point or two.

If you are unable to fit all your relevant information on one or two pages, certainly go ahead and add another page. If you expand to an additional page, try to fill at least half of the new page you added so that you don't have a mostly-blank page at the end.

Let me share a very important point about resumes: Many recruiters will spend *less than thirty seconds* with your resume before deciding to put it in an "advance" or "decline" pile. That's it. Just thirty seconds before a decision is made. That's why readability is so important.

In the next section, I'll talk about what happens in that short window of time—and how you can position things for best effect.

Resume Scans

You may think I'm exaggerating about people spending only thirty seconds reading your resume. However, studies have shown that some recruiters take only *six* seconds before making a decision!

That might seem completely unfair. After all, you may spend quite a while crafting your resume. You customize it slightly for each job. You triple-check it for errors. And then, in the end, someone spends just *six seconds* reading it?

Unfortunately, yes. That's sometimes how things often go—at least, for positions where there are many applicants.

When I am doing a high-level executive search, I may work for weeks to find just two or three qualified candidates. In that case, I'll spend plenty of time reading resumes very closely.

But if I have a job that garners hundreds of applicants, I need to process things very quickly. I personally try to spend at least a minute reading each resume. But other people will make a near-instantaneous decision based on a few elements that catch their eye.

Let me share an important note about how recruiters like me "scan" resumes on a first pass. Most of my counseling clients are surprised when I tell them this.

When I first read through a resume, I look at the following, in this order:

> Your name and your city of residence.
> The first couple sentences of your "summary" section.
> Your most recent job, plus just the first *one or two* experience bullets.
> Then I jump down to the your next job and read just the *first* bullet.
> Then I jump down to your education.

That's it.

Usually from that read, which takes a minute or less, I have a sense about whether someone is a great match, a possible match, or not a match at all.

Great matches I re-read in detail immediately. Possible matches go into a pile to hopefully review later. For non-matches, I'll still hold on to your resume for other positions. But the sorting takes place quickly.

An Example of a Resume Scan

To illustrate the scan process I described above, here's how a resume looks to me on a quick first-pass:

CAREER PSYCHOLOGY

Grace Washington
New York, NY
[I skip the rest of the contact info]

SUMMARY

Software Manager in the computer gaming industry with experience developing mass-market titles using both Unity and Unreal engines. Skilled at managing teams of up to 15 people, including software developers... *[I skip the rest]*

EXPERIENCE

Lead Producer: 3D Games
Braidwood Studios
2015 to present

- Led the production of six cross-platform titles on PC, Playstation, and Xbox systems which sold a combined 1.5 million units. Oversaw budgets up to $10 million per title and assisted with marketing campaign development.
- Managed a team of 12 direct reports, including...
- *[I skip the rest of the bullets]*

Associate Producer
Windpeak Systems
2000-2015

- Assisted with the development of three mobile games for both iOS and Android platforms, including prototyping, alpha builds, beta testing, and QA.
- *[I skip the rest of the bullets]*

[I skip the rest of the experience section]

EDUCATION

BS, Computer Science, 1993
University of Connecticut

[I skip anything else]

You can see from that "scan map" which parts of the resume are the most important: your summary, your most recent job and its first bullet or two, your next job and its first bullet, and your education.

Other recruiters may have slightly different scans. But it's likely that most of them will move through your resume like I do.

You can probably guess what we don't want to see: a resume that's difficult to read. When there's a resume that's unusually formatted due to design, layout, fonts, or simply organization of content, it prevents us from processing the resume quickly. When that happens, any possible matches get lost.

Unless you're a graphic designer, your resume should be in a standard, basic form. Graphic designers can (and should) play with creative flairs. For everyone else, though, simplicity and standard formats are crucial. Recruiters are simply processing too much to wrestle with anything unusual.

"But Dan," some of my clients have said, "I don't want to work for a company that can't take the proper time to read my resume."

Let me say that I wish that we recruiters had more time.

I personally would love to leisurely read through my stacks of resumes. I would enjoy delving into the details of everyone's backgrounds. After all, I'm a therapist; I'm always curious about people's lives. I enjoy studying career journeys.

But the truth is that most of us in the recruiting world are overwhelmed by multiple job openings with many applications crossing our desk every hour.

While we're reading resumes, we're scheduling interviews, trying to gather interview feedback, and fielding phone calls from people who were interviewed last week and need a decision immediately because they now have an offer with another company.

We just learned that the parameters for one of our jobs has changed, and now we need to cancel the interviews we set up, apologize to candidates, and start the entire search over from scratch.

We're in the middle of salary negotiations with someone via email. At the same time, we're waiting for calls back from candidates we cold-called earlier in the day, who may or may not get back to us, and for whom we'll need to drop everything if they do decide to call.

Most of us recruiters are dealing with all that, and more. That's why we are *very* grateful for resumes that help us see the relevant elements quickly. You are helping us enormously by presenting information that we can easily process.

Now that I've communicated how frenetic the daily life of a recruiter can be, and why an easily-readable resume is so important, let's talk about how to create that.

Resumes: The Early Sections

Let's begin at the top with your name. Your name can be simple; if you prefer that people call you Dan, you don't need to use Daniel on your resume. It's fine to have your name in a slightly larger font size than the rest of the resume if you wish.

Your resume should include a city and state. It's important for us recruiters to see how far you are from the company in case of a commute. We also may be searching databases using city names.

However, you're welcome to leave out your street address. In this era where people can find an old real estate listing and see the inside of your home, it may be wise to protect your privacy by simply listing city and state.

As I mentioned previously, I recommend to my clients that they set up a dedicated Gmail email account and Google Voice phone number for use on resumes. If you do create a new email and/or phone number, please make sure to forward or check messages regularly.

In the old days, people would include an "objective" at the top of the resume, right below their name and contact information. An objective would generally be a basic statement like:

> Objective: To obtain a job in manufacturing working with electronics.

There's nothing wrong with including an objective, but it usually doesn't add very much. It's also fairly old-school. A better approach is to include a "summary" section instead.

A summary is a one or two sentence overview of your background, skills, and what you are offering with your work. As you may recall from the previous section, the summary is the very first thing we read after your name and location. Therefore, it is your best chance to show a recruiter how you match with her job.

If your summary sounds like a fit for the job at hand, a recruiter will *have to* put you in the "possible match" group. There is no way that she will pass you by. You showed her, right up front, that you're a potential fit. That is why the summary is one of your best places to catch your reader's attention.

I encourage you to slightly customize your summary for each individual job application. It only takes a minute or two to rewrite these couple of sentences. It's worth the time to modify your summary on an application-by-application basis in order to help the matches pop.

Let me share a few examples of what I mean by a summary.

Let's imagine that you're applying for an Office Manager job with a small, high-tech company. Part of the job involves working with an outside IT firm. Your summary might say:

Versatile Office Manager with experience working for small, fast-paced companies. Skilled at working with technology, including management of IT functions.

As soon as a recruiter sees a summary like that, she will say, "Wow! This person might be a great fit!" She will then read your resume very closely and carefully.

You might have actually spent a good part of your career working in non-technology fields, or at large companies. But your summary shows a potential match for this specific job you're applying for: the small companies, the technology focus, and even the IT piece.

Those matches are what a recruiter will be looking for. There they are, right up front.

Here's another example. Let's say that you're interested in a sales job at a car dealership. You don't have any experience selling cars. However, in order to show some potential matches, your summary says:

Sales professional with experience negotiating and closing high-value deals. Skilled at building relationships, including relationships with walk-in customers.

Car sales aren't listed there. However, a recruiter will see "high value deals," "negotiation" skills, and work with "walk-in customers." Those are all extremely relevant. After all, you will be selling expensive cars to walk-in customers, and there will be price negotiations. There might be a great match here.

Your summary is one of the most important parts of your resume—especially if you customize it to show potential matches.

Now, do you *have to* include a summary section? No, it's not essential. Only half of the resumes I receive have one.

But can it help? Yes indeed—more than almost anything else, given that it's one of the first things we recruiters see. I highly recommend including one.

Resumes: The Experience Section

Let's now move on to the heart of your resume: your work experience.

A typical "experience" section of your resume will list your past jobs in reverse chronological order, with your most recent job first. Each job should start with the following header:

The company you worked at
Your job title
Dates of employment

It's fine to put your title before the company, if you prefer that order. Some people also include the location of the company.

If the companies you worked for aren't well known, you can add a short one-sentence description of what each company does. This will help your reader understand your line of work.

After the company, title, and date information comes a series of four to seven bullets that describe your work responsibilities and accomplishments at each job.

I've seen resumes with only two or three bullets for each job; that is probably too little information. I've also seen resumes with eight or more bullets; that is too many. A reader simply can't process that much information.

As a reminder, a recruiter may only read the *first bullet or two* of your most recent job, and then the *first bullet* of your next job. At least on a first pass. So like the summary, those are the elements that are the most important.

Please consider re-ordering and re-writing those first few bullets for every job you apply for. The matches between your experience and the job you're applying for should pop right out.

Bullet Format

To maximize the impact of your bullets, I recommend that you use a "verb—detail—results (if available)" format.

Bullets should start with a verb, and then describe your work and accomplishments. It's helpful to include some quantified detail if possible. If you can add specific *results* to a few bullets as well, that's great.

Let me share a few examples of bullets the follow this format:

(Verb:) Managed (detail:) a team of ten people to conduct quality checks on manufactured products, (result:) resulting in a cost savings of $50,000 per year.

(Verb:) Provided (detail:) addiction recovery services to over forty in-patient clients, (result:) leading to long-term substance use reduction in 75% of the population.

(Verb:) Taught (detail:) five classes of beginning algebra with an average class size of thirty students. (Result:) Helped to raise test scores 22% over prior year.

Each of those followed a "verb—detail—result" format. As a bonus, all of them included some numbers in the detail, and each ended with a measurable result. (Note that the third example has the result in a *second* sentence within the same bullet. That's fine to do.)

Now, you certainly don't need to list results in every bullet. But results give a strong "kicker" to your descriptions. They describe precisely what you accomplished, and how your efforts impacted the company or the public. This gives significant weight to your description.

"Dan," you might be thinking, "I have absolutely no idea how to measure my results at work. In fact, I don't think I'm getting results most of the time!"

That's fine; that's the case for many of us. Certainly don't feel pressure to come up with results for every bullet. However, my guess is that you can sprinkle in at least one or two impact statements about your work.

These can be general things like:

Managed a coffee shop, including all advertising efforts, *leading to an increase in traffic and revenue.*

Designed a new user manual for a manufacturing client, *resulting in improved customer satisfaction.*

Edited thirty books in both fiction and non-fiction fields. *Two of these books reached local bestseller lists.*

If you do include results, be prepared to discuss them in an interview. What type of advertising did you do at the coffee shop? How did your user manual improve customer satisfaction? How did the editing help the books land on bestseller lists?

You did—and do—make an impact with your work every day. By all means, claim the credit you are due! Resumes are not the place to be overly modest. If you can describe how your work helped to produce results, your impact will come across in a very powerful way.

Let me now highlight one of the most crucial parts of resume writing: including relevant keywords. Keywords are what recruiters are looking for in computer-based searches. Part of resume writing involves skillfully weaving keywords into your bullets.

Try to think like a recruiter when you're writing your bullets. What are some unique terms that recruiters might be searching on? What are some phrases that they might be looking for? To help answer this, you can take a look at several job ads in your field. What are some unique words that are included in the ads?

Try to weave those keywords—and related ones—into your bullets. Recall the electrical engineering search that I mentioned in chapter four. I'm looking for keywords like "FPGA" and "Zynq" and "embedded systems." Resumes that contain those keywords in the bullets will pop up on my list.

There are undoubtedly many unique terms, phrases, acronyms, and systems in your line of work (or the line of work you want to get into). Try to weave those naturally into your bullets.

Resumes: The Rest

As a reminder, the most important parts of your resume are:

1. the summary at the top,
2. the first two bullets of your most recent job, and
3. the first bullet of your next most recent job.

Those are the parts that many recruiters will focus on in a first-pass read.

After those, I myself usually skip down and read the education section at the end of the resume. For technical or medical jobs, this section is crucial. If a degree in mechanical engineering is required, I need to confirm that.

For most other jobs, the education section may be less important—but it can still be impactful, especially if you include relevant trainings and certifications in addition to any formal degrees.

It's not typical to list your high school in your education section. However, if you attended college for any length of time (even if you didn't complete a degree), you're welcome to list the college. Folks without degrees can use a statement like, "Completed classes in business management," or something similar.

Please also include any trainings and certifications in this section. Especially in information technology and medical fields, certifications are often valued as much as degrees.

Now, what about sections like "interests," "volunteer experience," and "skills" that many resumes include at the end? Are those worth including?

My answer is: sure, an "interests" or "volunteer experience" section is fine if you have extra space. You're welcome to include those if you have room. They can give us interviewers a great jumping-off point for conversations. ("You're a rock climber? Me too! Where do you like to climb?") However, these sections are optional and should not be included if you're struggling to fit more important information.

A "skills" section at the end of the resume is common. For technical people, this often includes programming languages or computer systems. Feel free to include this section if you have specific skills that are relevant to the job at hand.

A Sample Resume

Let me now pull all of this together by sharing a sample resume. The person in this example is applying for a marketing job with a focus on internet-based work.

After I present this, I'll identify some important things that she did in her resume.

Jane Adams
Denver, Colorado
(303) 555-1000
janeadams@fairexec.com

SUMMARY

Marketing Manager with extensive experience leading internet-based advertising and marketing efforts, including email campaigns, video production, website search engine optimization, and online advertising placement.

EXPERIENCE

Winterhold Mountain Properties
Marketing Manager
2018—present

Winterhold Mountain Properties is a real estate holding company for residential properties throughout Colorado.

- Led all marketing activities for the sale of properties, including management of digital campaigns. Helped increase revenue by 45% and reduce time-on-market of properties from 45 to 22 days.
- Produced a series of videos highlighting properties which were viewed by more than 10,000 people. 25% of new customers reported viewing these videos.
- Worked with an outside SEO firm to optimize keywords and copy for company website, resulting in a 15% increase in website traffic year-over-year.
- Launched monthly email campaigns using Constant Contact. Wrote content for email blasts and worked with design firms to create layouts using HTML/CSS.

- Managed advertising campaigns on Google Ads and Facebook Marketplace, including analysis and A/B tests.
- Built relationships with outside vendors, including outside marketing agencies.

Riverwood Productions
Marketing Specialist
2014-2018

Riverwood Productions is a marketing agency that specializes in print-based advertising.

- Helped the company to launch its first major digital marketing campaign, as an adjunct to traditional print advertising efforts. The combined approach led to a 30% increase in sales inquiries for the client.
- Worked with a team of designers and copywriters to develop ads for placement in magazines and other media.
- Managed relationships with editors, publicists, public relations specialists, and other industry insiders in the publishing and advertising worlds.
- Helped develop new clientele by working with account managers to produce marketing collateral.

EDUCATION AND TRAINING

University of Colorado at Boulder
B.A., Business Administration

Degree program included classes on marketing communication, digital production, and advertising. Also completed trainings in Adobe Photoshop, InDesign, Illustrator, Premier, and After Effects. Certified user of Salesforce.com CRM system.

Let me go through Jane's resume and point out a few things that she did very well.

To begin, her resume is in a standard format, easy to read, and filled with relevant information. That is the best foundation upon which to build. Given that she's in marketing, she can add a few design flairs if she'd like.

Because she's applying for a position that is focused on internet-based work, she customized her summary to highlight that. If a recruiter were to *only* read Jane's summary and nothing else, he would have to place Jane in the "possible match" group. Jane showed the recruiter, right up front, that there's a potentially strong fit. There's no way for him to pass her by.

Jane also included a great deal of relevant detail—including specific results—in her first few bullets. Along with the summary, these bullets are the most important parts of the resume. She highlighted some excellent matches for the job.

Because both of her companies are relatively unknown and have unusual names, Jane did the recruiter a favor by summarizing what each of the companies do. Without that information, he might be delayed and confused while trying to figure out what type of industry Jane was in.

Jane's second job was with a company that primarily did print-based work. The job she's applying for, by contrast, is focused on internet-based work. Because of that, she chose to start with a bullet about helping her company develop a blended print/internet approach.

Even if this was a small part of her work, it is nonetheless an extremely relevant element for this particular job opening. She put that front and center.

She also skillfully wove keywords into her bullets: things like "A/B testing" (a way of measuring ad effectiveness), companies like Constant Contact (email marketing) and Google Ads (online ads), and HTML/CSS (the language for creating websites.)

In addition, she used the acronym "SEO" and also wrote out "search engine optimization." She covered both formats.

Note that Jane used only years, and not months, on her dates of employment. I recommend this. It keeps things simple, and also helps to cover up any gaps. She also included some relevant trainings and a certification in her last section.

This is an easy-to-read resume filled with relevant items that pop up quickly. That is what we're aiming for. Resumes don't need to be fancy; they simply need to highlight matches.

The Cover Letter

Let me now move on to part two of this chapter: the cover letter.

The majority of the resumes I receive have no cover letter at all, or just a few sentences. I'm used to this; it doesn't bother me. But when I see that someone took time to write a relevant cover letter, it strengthens the application.

I *strongly* recommend that you include a brief cover letter with your resume when you apply for jobs. It's worth the extra time to create.

I'm going to share a format that I call "Dan's cover letter." This isn't industry-standard. (There is no standard.) But it's what I most like to see. Most recruiters probably feel the same.

My cover letter format is only three paragraphs long. Each paragraph has just two or three sentences.

Here is the format:

1. Paragraph One: Introduce yourself, and name the job you're interested in.
2. Paragraph Two: Highlight some matches between your background and the job.
3. Paragraph Three: Wrap-up and express your interest in having a conversation.

That's it. Just three paragraphs.

Remember that many recruiters will spend only seconds on your resume. The same is true with your cover letter as well.

I've had numerous counseling clients who found it extremely difficult to write such a short cover letter. They wanted to make a strong sales pitch by including pages of detail. I always recommend against this.

To be safe, assume that you have no more than 15 seconds of the reader's attention. Most readers will skip the final paragraph completely, so your first two paragraphs are what really matters. Your goal is to name the job you're interested in, and highlight the top matches. That's all you need to do.

Let's return to Jane in marketing. If Jane were to write a cover letter using my three-paragraph format, it might look like this:

Dear Hiring Manager:

I was delighted to see the opening for an Internet Marketing Manager with your company. As a marketing professional with experience managing digital campaigns, I would like to submit the attached resume.

In my current role as a Marketing Manager, I lead email marketing efforts, create videos, optimize websites for SEO, and manage online ad placements. In my previous role at an agency, I helped the company to launch its first blended internet/print campaign.

I am available to speak with you at your convenience. Please call or text me on my cell phone at (303) 555-1000 or email me at janeadams@fairexec.com. Thank you for your consideration.

Sincerely,
Jane Adams

That's it. Anything longer will probably get ignored.

Let's look at what Jane did. In her first sentence, she named the job that she's applying for. This is important. Many recruiters are receiving applications for multiple positions. They will need to know which role you're interested in.

The second paragraph is what really matters. Jane knows from the job ad that the company is seeking someone with email, SEO, and online ad experience. She highlighted those up front.

The last paragraph is just a polite wrap-up.

An Alternative

A slight alternative to this format—which is even easier to read—is to convert the second paragraph to bullets. In this alternative format, the three paragraphs might look like this:

Dear Hiring Manager:

I was delighted to see the opening for an Internet Marketing Manager with your company. As a marketing professional with experience managing digital campaigns, I would like to submit the attached resume.

My current and past responsibilities have included:
- leading email marketing efforts
- creating videos
- optimizing websites for SEO
- managing online ad placements
- launching a blended internet/print campaign.

I am available to speak with you at your convenience. Please call or text me on my cell phone at (303) 555-1000 or email me at janeadams@fairexec.com. Thank you for your consideration.

Sincerely,
Jane Adams

It's almost identical to the first version, but it uses bullets to highlight matches. I personally like this format a great deal.

My career counseling clients often struggle with cover letter writing until they begin to practice with this simple format. Then things become quite easy. You can quickly modify the first and second paragraphs for each new job. The third paragraph doesn't need to change at all.

Although you're welcome to craft whatever type of cover letter you'd like, I invite you to experiment with this format. This style is quick to write, and quick to read—and as I've stated, speed of processing is essential.

Cover Letters: The Exception

There is one exception to my cover letter rule. If you are applying for a job that is *not* in-line with your background, the cover letter becomes a crucial tool for helping a recruiter see why you're a fit.

In these situations, feel free to expand things slightly. (Just slightly, though!)

Let's say, for example, that you have primarily worked as a bookstore manager. You are now interested in crossing over into the hotel industry. You don't have any experience in hospitality, although you have some very relevant skills.

Here's how a slightly longer cover letter might look for a job as a hotel desk manager:

Dear Hiring Manager:

I am very interested in your opening for a Hotel Front Desk Manager. Over the course of my career, I have interacted with thousands of customers, managed teams of up to five people, and held responsibility for off-hour issues.

Your role appeals to me because I am eager to join a team

in the hospitality industry. I am confident that my management experience will cross-over to a hotel environment.

My work in retail management has focused on customer satisfaction and responding to challenges. I have resolved conflict situations, managed infrastructure issues including electrical and plumbing problems, and been "on call" in the event that team members needed assistance.

I am available to speak with you at your convenience. Please call or text me on my cell phone at (212) 555-3000 or email me at tanya@fairexec.com. Thank you for your consideration.

Sincerely,
Tanya Jefferson

As you can see, Tanya slightly expanded past the brief three-paragraph format in order to clarify that she wants to cross over to a hospitality environment. She also highlighted some relevant skills for that new industry.

If a recruiter only looks at her resume, the matches might get missed. After all, Tanya is coming from a bookstore environment, rather than a hotel.

However, her cover letter confirms that she wants to make a change, and highlights why she's a great fit. She has worked with customers, she has managed teams, she has been on-call during off hours. She has even handled electrical and plumbing issues—helpful experience for a hotel manager!

Hopefully the recruiter or hiring manager will read through this cover letter and see the enthusiasm and matches. The cover letter is still short and sweet. We only expanded it by a paragraph.

Cover Letters: Final Points

Let me conclude the cover letter section with a few important suggestions.

I encourage you to both "over apply" and "under apply" for jobs in order to expand your options. Cover letters can help with both of these situations.

Here's what I mean by over and under applying:

You can apply for jobs that are slightly *below* your experience level, and make a pitch for the company to expand the role. You can confirm in your cover letter that your experience matches the job description, and also express that you bring additional skills to the table.

I have had job applicants say to me, "Dan, I can do everything on your position description. But I can also do these other things as well. Would you be interested in expanding this role to include those responsibilities?" Although that's a conversation best suited for a phone call, your cover letter can tee up that pitch.

You can also apply for jobs that are slightly *above* your experience level—jobs which contain skills that you have not yet gained. In that case, the cover letter is a perfect place to highlight the matches that you do have.

Name the matches, and then if you do have a follow-up conversation with a recruiter, you can clarify to them that you will need to "come up to speed" on several other parts of the position description.

I have filled job openings with both of these types of applicants. In the first scenario, the company chose to expand a role to match the candidate's higher-level skills (and salary). In the second scenario, the company was willing to train the new employee on aspects of the job that she hadn't been exposed to.

In both of these cases, the cover letter can help to move you on to the clarifying conversations.

As a final note, I myself like to see the cover letter directly in the body of an email—not as a separate attachment.

I can't tell you how many times I've received a completely blank email with nothing but two attachments: "resume" and "cover letter." In those cases, I skip the cover letter entirely. After all, if I'm going to open a separate document, it's going to be the resume!

For best results, copy your cover letter right into the body of the email. Then attach your resume as a PDF (preferred) or a Microsoft Word document. Send that off, give yourself a pat on the back, and then move on to additional applications.

Of course, please check each new version of your resume for typos, misspellings, alignment issues, and grammatical errors. You may want to ask a friend or family member to take a second look for you.

One thing to keep in mind about resumes and cover letters is that they're simply designed to open the door to further conversations. All you need do is highlight the matches between your abilities and the job description. That is the primary purpose of a resume and cover letter.

Online Applications

Before moving on to the Q&As for this topic, let me briefly discuss online applications.

In general, small companies keep the application process simple. They usually say, "Please email a cover letter and resume to careers@fairexec.com" or something similar. You can then do what I recommended above: Copy your cover letter into the body of an email, attach your resume, and hit send.

However, large companies and organizations often use what is called an "Applicant Tracking System," or ATS. An ATS is essentially a database system that stores your resume, cover letter, and other information for the company. Almost every large company employs an ATS these days. Smaller high-tech companies are beginning to use them as well.

Applicant tracking systems are great for companies; they allow recruiters to sort, organize, and search resumes easily. But for applicants, they can be frustrating. They often require you to enter a great deal of your information manually into forms. Even if the system tries to import elements of your resume automatically, you will still need to double-check and correct things.

Here's what I say to my career counseling clients about ATS's: They will probably only add 15 minutes to the application process. It's best to just flow with things.

Also, many other applicants will become annoyed with the ATS forms and quit the process. This is good news for you, as it means that your application will have less competition.

Once you've entered your information into an ATS for a specific company, you may not need to re-enter it for additional job openings at that same company. Often it's a one-time thing.

In addition, there is a different type of online application system that is the complete opposite of a form-based ATS system. In this other system, all you need to do is hit a *single button* to apply for a job.

For example, if you have a profile or resume on LinkedIn or Indeed, you can simply click a link to apply for a job. Your LinkedIn profile or Indeed resume is already stored. You hit a button, and we recruiters receive your information.

Those systems are great. However, when using them, you still will benefit by attaching a cover letter and a full resume. Most recruiters give more weight to applications that have those attached—after all, it shows that you took some extra time and are genuinely interested in the role.

Let me now move on to some common questions about resumes, cover letters, and the application process.

CHAPTER SEVEN

Resumes, Cover Letters, and Applications: A Deeper Look

As a reminder, your resume is simply designed to open a door. Its primary function is to show the matches between your background and the job you're interested in. For best results, you can keep your resume simple, clear, and in a standard format.

I recommend that you customize the summary and first few bullets of your resume for each job application. I also recommend that you include a brief cover letter. If your resume and cover letter clearly show why you're a fit for the job, you make it very easy for a recruiter to move you along in the process.

Let me now share some questions I've received about writing resumes and cover letters, and sending in job applications.

Q: I am over 50 and I'm concerned about age discrimination. Is there anything I can do to protect myself from that?

A: Certainly. Even though employment discrimination against protected classes (age, race, and many other categories) is illegal, it is nonetheless common. Particularly age discrimination.

Let me share a few things you can do to reduce the chance of this impacting you.

First, you don't need to include the year of your college degree if you have one. In the past, everyone was expected to list a degree date on their resume. Now, many people leave that out.

If you look back to Jane Adams's sample resume from the last chapter, you'll see that she listed her college degree without a year. You might not have even noticed that at the time, as it appears quite normal.

You're also not required to include the early parts of your work experience. Many people only list their past 15 to 20 years of work. They might add, "Earlier Experience:" at the bottom, along with a summary of early-career roles. Or they might simply cap the list at 15 or 20 years.

Let's return for a moment to the resume of Jane Adams. Her work experience on her resume started in the year 2014. She didn't list a date of graduation from college.

Did Jane graduate in 2014, and this was her first job? Or is she a 2004 graduate who has ten years of experience that are not on the resume? Or did she graduate in 1984, and begin her career thirty years after college?

No one will know. Everyone will probably assume that she's a 2014 graduate, but no one can know for sure. And most people in human resources won't even try to hint around with questions about graduation dates, knowing the potential for age discrimination.

If you do omit a graduation date or your early work experience, it's best to double-check that your LinkedIn and Facebook profiles also omit those as well. Otherwise, a company can check dates by simply looking at your online profiles.

Now, let me share a couple of caveats. First, some Applicant Tracking Systems will force you to enter your year of graduation and your full work history. You should not lie if asked for required information.

If you are given a job offer, your information from the ATS may be submitted for verification during a background check. If any deception is discovered, your offer may be withdrawn. It's best to be honest about information you're required to give.

As another caveat, I have talked to a few executives over the years who considered it evasive when candidates didn't list their entire work history. The norms are shifting, and these executives might not yet be up with the times. But some hiring managers do expect a full work history on a resume.

In order to protect yourself, you can consider including that "Earlier experience:" line along with a general summary. In most cases, that will probably be sufficient to cover any bases.

Your primary goal can be to get past any age-related bias in the initial resume screening, and move toward a conversation between you and the company. Once you are talking to people, you can impress them with your enthusiasm, experience, wisdom, and other gifts.

Q: I've had several periods in my life where I was out of work for a while. Is there anything I can do about these "gaps" on my resume?

A: Yes indeed. One of the simplest techniques is to only use years on your resume—not months and years. Most recruiters don't care about months anyway. By using years, you can reduce any gaps.

As an example, let's say that you were employed from January 2016 to February 2019. Then you were out of work for a year and a half. Then you started a new position in September 2020.

If you list only the years, your resume will say:

| First Company | 2016-2019 |
| Second Company | 2020-present |

That looks pretty good to me! Most recruiters won't blink an eye over that. You successfully closed an 18 month work gap by removing months.

The other common technique is to state that you were a "consultant," "contractor," "freelancer" or some other term during non-employed times in your career. Don't lie about this, of course. It will backfire if you're inventing things.

However, let's say that you helped your friend's side business from time to time when you were unemployed. Would your friend be OK with you stating that you assisted him as a consultant during that time? If so, you can add that to your resume in order to fill in a gap.

If you did side projects for other businesses—even if you didn't get paid much—you can consider putting a summary of those activities on a resume. We HR folks know that if someone was laid-off from a job and has been working as a "consultant" for several months, she has probably been primarily job searching. But it does fill in gaps, and we see it all the time.

Please note that there may be some hiring managers who consider these techniques to be borderline deceptive. You will have to use your own wisdom about whether or not to use them. However, I have seen thousands of resumes that were filling in gaps using these methods.

If you have a long gap (say, more than a year or two), it's not unusual to give a brief explanation. I have seen resumes that stated, "Took a sabbatical to care for a family member," or "Pursued educational opportunities during this time," or similar types of explanations. I personally don't ask people about these. However, other recruiters might delve in a bit, so be prepared to discuss.

As I mentioned earlier, please make sure that your LinkedIn profile dates match the resume. (You can delete months from LinkedIn, and only use years.)

When recruiters see discrepancies on dates between resumes and LinkedIn, it raises concerns.

Q: I'm thinking about hiring a professional resume writer to create my resume. Do you think that's a good idea?

A: Sure, that's fine. However, please add your own personal touch to the resume once the writer gets done with it.

I can't tell you how many professionally written resumes I've seen that look exactly the same. I mean *exactly* the same, down to the design flairs and all. They're often easy to spot. When I see a resume written by a third party, I do sometimes wonder if the person is comfortable creating his own written work.

In my career counseling practice, I don't write resumes for people; I help my clients to write their resumes themselves. In this way, they end up using their own phrasing and language—not mine. In the same way, you might want to consider giving your professionally written resume a slight re-write so that it sounds like it's coming from you.

I do want to share one strange thing that I see on many professionally written resumes. It is this:

For some reason, many of these resumes include a bunch of job titles at the top of the first page, often accompanied by a list of keywords. I am not sure who came up with this format. It can be very confusing.

For example, let's say that I'm working on a search for an Accounting Manager, and I receive a resume from a candidate.

If the resume has a banner at the top that says:

CFO • VP Finance • Controller • Accounting Manager

...then I'm not sure what to think of all these titles.

Is this person actually wanting a Chief Financial Officer role? (A CFO is a much higher role than the opening I have.) Will this person be looking for a CFO role, even if she joins my company as an Accounting Manager?

If the goal is to indicate that the candidate is open to various roles, that doesn't really help her. She is applying for this one specific position. I want to know that she's excited about my job!

My guess is that this style harkens back to an old time where you had to custom-print a single resume, and then use that one resume for a wide variety of job applications. Back when you couldn't easily customize a resume, perhaps it made sense to list a bunch of titles. But today, that list is a distraction.

Along the same lines, some professionally written resumes have a "skills" section at the top of the first page that is just a big list of words in multiple columns. This isn't a good use of crucial space. If you include a skills list, it should be near the end of the resume.

If you do hire a professional resume writer, you might want to hire someone who has worked in recruiting and human resources. Most people in the HR world will give you the same advice: Keep your resume simple and clear, highlight relevant matches, and use a standard format.

Q: I'm helping my daughter put together a resume for the first time. She just graduated from college, and has only worked in child care. Do you have any suggestions for someone in this situation?

A: I wouldn't worry too much about the specific resume content if your daughter is right out of school. Very few people in her situation will have significant work experience. The resume will be more of a demonstration of her organizational and writing skills.

Having said that, she may want to list her education first (rather than last) on the resume. She can boost the education section by listing coursework, lab work, special projects, and so forth. If she has a great GPA, she can list it. She can also include trainings and certifications like CPR.

Even though her only experience is in child care, she may be able to come up with some colorful bullets for that work.

Did she do outreach to families in your community about her child care services? If so, she can describe that. Her outreach skills might be quite impressive to a company.

Did she create educational opportunities for the kids she was caring for—perhaps visits to museums or other field trips? If so, that's great to include.

Is there anything that distinguishes her offerings from other child care providers? If so, she can describe those elements.

You don't want things to sound puffed-up, of course. But in truth, your daughter has very likely exhibited some impressive skills in her child care work. Don't be shy about highlighting details.

Q: Should I list references on my resume?

A: It's best not to list references on the resume itself. If the company would like references from you, they'll ask.

I've seen some publicly-posted resumes that list names, cell phone numbers, and personal emails of references for everyone to see. My guess is that references don't want to have their contact information broadcasted this way!

You can wait and see if the company even needs references. If so, they might have certain people they'd like to talk to (for example, your past supervisors). You can wait for their guidance on this.

Q: You mentioned that there were some "resume tips" that you disagreed with. Can you give a few examples?

A: Sure. Here are some tips I've read in various articles, along with my responses:

"Use a non-chronological resume format to stand out."

Please no! I recommend using a reverse-chronology format with your most recent job listed first. I don't recommend a "functional resume" or other style unless you're in a *very* unusual situation (for example, if you haven't worked at all for the past 20 years). If a recruiter can't process your resume quickly, she'll likely move on to the next one.

"Limit your resume to one page."

Only if you are fairly new to the workforce, or if you're in an industry which expects one-page resumes (including some law firms.) If you're mid-career or later, you have far too many interesting accomplishments to squeeze everything onto one page.

"Start your resume with a list of your skills."

This isn't my preference. A list of keywords at the top of the resume wastes the most important section. Instead, create a customized two-sentence summary, and weave in skills that match the job you're applying for.

"Consider including a photo on your resume."

I don't recommend this. First of all, photos on resumes are very unusual—at least in the United States. Second, we in the HR field are working very hard to remain fact-based and unbiased in our hiring decisions. We want to absorb your factual career information—not be influenced by your appearance.

"It's OK to leave out dates on your jobs."

No, employment dates are crucial. It's fine to leave off the date of your college degree, especially if you're concerned about age discrimination. But please make sure to include years for each one of your jobs. If we can't find those, it makes your resume very difficult to follow.

"Consider listing your education first."

If you are coming out of college and have limited work experience, that's fine. Otherwise, we're used to seeing the education at the bottom.

"Include your GPA in your education section."

I only recommend this if it's over 3.5.

"List your social media accounts in your contact section."

This is risky. A LinkedIn URL is fine. However, pointing us to your Facebook, Instagram, and other accounts will probably not help unless you use them strictly for professional activities.

"Include phrases copied directly from the job posting."

Although I've written at length about highlighting matches, it's best to *not* copy exact phrases from the job description verbatim. When people do that, it comes across as manipulative. It's best to simply describe the matches in ways that accurately reflect your background.

"Start with an objective at the top."

I recommend using a summary instead of an objective. The summary should be slightly customized to the job at hand, and show the matches with your background.

"Use color to make your resume stand out."

One accent color, used judiciously, can add some flair. But it's best not to blast the viewer with multiple colors or brightly colored banners. It distracts us from the actual content of your resume.

"Include charts and other graphical elements on your resume."

I don't recommend this, as it can make the resume hard to follow. Let the bullets listing your accomplishments be the part that stands out.

Those are just some of the suggestions I disagree with.

However, to be fair, I can recall numerous top candidates I've come across who *did* have colorful resumes, or lists of skills at the top, or had a photo included. None of these are make-or-break things—except for the overall format. It's best in almost all cases to use a standard, reverse-chronology style.

Q: I feel intimidated by job ads that have an "about you" section and say things like, "You are boundlessly creative," "You are a genius at this skill," and "You inspire whatever team you work for." I figure that I'm going to disappoint them if I apply. How do you interpret ads like these?

A: Those ads are usually written by marketing people, or by recruiters who are fairly new and are trying to be creative. Any experienced recruiter knows that a job ad should feel welcoming, encouraging, and down-to-earth—not intimidating. After all, we want as many people as possible to be interested.

My suggestion is to apply for anything that interests you, as long as it's in the ballpark. Then move on to your next application without another thought. Don't read too much into the language or tone of the job ad. It's unlikely that the ads you referenced were written by the hiring manager who you'll be working for.

If you end up talking to someone in the company, you can be as honest as you like. You can give an authentic portrayal of your skills and personality. If they truly want a boundlessly creative genius who inspires every team they work for—well, good luck!

I myself would not want to work for a company that has an attitude of "only the best of the best work here." However, once you actually talk to people at the company, you might find that they are very humble, warm, and welcoming—even if the language of the job ad indicated otherwise. I encourage you to go ahead and apply.

Q: Usually when I apply for a job and don't hear back, I feel like I've failed. It makes me not want to try again. Is there anything I can do about those feelings of failure?

A: This is a very common experience. You are certainly not alone. I have felt those feelings myself, and almost everyone I know has as well.

Let me introduce a concept from psychology called "locus of control." I will return to this idea later in this book as well.

Imagine a circle that surrounds you. Things that are *inside* that circle are under your control. Things *outside* the circle are outside your control.

For example, your choice about what to eat for lunch is inside the circle. It is under your control. Whether or not it will rain today is outside of your circle. It is outside your control.

The interesting thing is that *everyone draws a different sized circle*. Some people believe they are in control of almost everything in their lives—and thus responsible for those things. This creates a sense of empowerment, but also generates a great deal of pressure.

Other people are the opposite. They have a very small circle of things that seem to be within their control. This removes pressure, but leads to feelings of powerlessness.

You may want to examine your own locus of control circle as it relates to your job applications.

If you believe that you're largely in control of "getting an interview"—and that doesn't happen—you will probably feel a sense of failure. You may feel shame and pressure to figure out what you did wrong. This can create a painful emotional storm.

On the other hand, if you believe that you have *no* ability to tip the scales toward getting an interview, you might believe that it's pointless to try. You might feel as though you are invisible and ignored—that you're just a leaf being blown by the wind of life. This can also be emotionally distressing.

The ideal is to draw a circle that is empowering but not pressuring. You might want to adjust your locus of control circle accordingly.

Can you make a strong pitch on a job application by highlighting matches between your background and the job opening? Yes indeed! That's certainly in your control.

Can you force a company to *respond* to your application? No. That's outside your control.

Can you express your enthusiasm about this job opening? Yes, definitely.

Can you control how people will *react* to your enthusiasm? No, you can't.

Can you move on peacefully to a new application once you've sent this one in? Yes, you sure can.

Can you force things to "click" with this company and "get a job"? No, that's not in your control.

By redrawing your locus of control circles (which are nothing but beliefs in the mind), you can increase your sense of empowerment, and also reduce feelings of pressure and failure.

I encourage you to experiment with this and see what you find. I'll build on this idea further in chapter twelve, where I discuss increasing your happiness at work.

•

Let me wrap-up by summarizing the main points I covered on this topic.

Your resume and cover letter are written for one primary purpose: to highlight matches between your background and the job at hand. It's important for your resume and cover letter to be easily readable. We want the job/skill matches to pop out quickly.

Standard formats are best. We recruiters are reading through resumes at a breakneck pace, and anything that slows us down is unhelpful. I encourage you to use a normal, reverse-chronology format for your resume with your most recent job listed first. Keep adequate margins and use a standard font that is not too small.

Take time to customize the first several bullets for each job application. Also customize the summary section at the top of your resume. Use these sections to highlight the most relevant matches between your accomplishments and the job you're applying for.

A good format for bullets is "verb—description—results (if possible)." You don't have to include results in every bullet, but try to include some in the first few. Quantified results with numbers are ideal. However, even general results like, "resulting in increased sales" are helpful.

For the cover letter, you can follow my three-paragraph format. The first paragraph introduces you and names the job you're interested in. The second paragraph highlights matches. The third paragraph wraps up, and is just a formality.

Recruiters will likely spend between six and thirty seconds on your resume and cover letter. Showing us the matches right up front ensures that you'll get a deeper look.

Let's now move on to the big step: the interview.

CHAPTER EIGHT

Interviews

In this chapter I'll be covering not only the traditional interview, but the entire flow of communication that takes place between submitting your application and receiving a job offer. Every exchange you have with a company is part of the process. Each "touch" can be important.

Interviewing for jobs can feel intimidating at times. Let me share what I tell my counseling clients: For many people, three of the most stressful experiences in life are first dates, public speaking, and... job interviews.

Because of that, I want to reassure you that it's OK to feel nervous during the interview process. It's normal and expected.

You don't have to come across as "cool" during an interview. You can simply try to be friendly and helpful. Those are the qualities that most companies are looking for—not some kind of slick smoothness.

The most challenging part of interviewing for most people is the fear of rejection, and the anxiety that comes with that. In this chapter, I will share a number of techniques from the world of cognitive behavioral therapy that can help to make the emotional aspects of the interview process easier.

For now, though, let me state once again: If you simply focus on being friendly and helpful during the interview process, good things will likely happen. Most organizations are not looking for cool characters. Instead, they're looking for kind people.

"But Dan, you have no idea!" some of my clients say. "I fall apart in interviews. I get completely flustered. My mind goes blank and the whole thing is terribly awkward."

Let me share that I have struggled with shyness and fears of disapproval throughout my own life. That is one of the reasons I became a therapist. It is also one of the reasons I enjoy recruiting—the process of constantly reaching out to people (and dealing with "rejection" every day) helps me to work with these tendencies.

So although I haven't been in your exact shoes, I've probably had some similar experiences to what you are fearing. In fact, many of my interpersonal encounters were probably as awkward and anxiety-filled as anything you're anticipating.

Can you guess what happened to me because of those awkward encounters? Not a whole lot. I didn't impress the person I was talking with, but so be it. There's always another encounter to be had.

Let me ask you to consider a scenario. If you were the owner of a small business, and you were interviewing two candidates, which of the following two people would you choose?

> Person A is honest, friendly, and somewhat nervous in an interview.
> Person B comes across as smooth and confident, but doesn't necessarily strike you as trustworthy and kind.

Which of those people would you want on your team? Who would you choose to hire?

Every business owner I know would choose Person A.

I share all this because interviewing is really about relationship-building. And relationships are built on authenticity and trustworthiness.

I don't want you to feel pressured to fight your emotions in an attempt to impress people and generate a specific image.

Instead, I encourage you to simply focus on offering kindness, friendliness, and helpfulness. Most people will react very positively to that.

The First Interview

To begin this chapter, let me discuss what a typical interview process looks like. If you're new to job interviewing, or have been away from the job search for a while, this section will outline what you can expect.

The first person who responds to your job application will very likely be one of three people:

1. a recruiter,
2. a human resources generalist, or
3. a hiring manager.

Let me describe each of these three people.

Recruiters like me are considered human resources "specialists." We do just one thing: We find people for job openings. We don't deal with other aspects of HR like benefits administration, workplace conflicts, or employee trainings.

Your first contact with a company might be a recruiter. If so, please know that *our entire purpose is to fill jobs*—and we would love it if you are the one for this role!

There are other people called human resources "generalists" who handle a broader array of responsibilities. These people are involved in recruiting, but not exclusively so.

Small companies can usually only afford a single HR staff member, so it's quite likely that a generalist will be the first person you talk to. Larger companies usually have recruiters on staff who will handle communication with you.

Neither recruiters nor HR generalists will make the ultimate decision about whether you will be hired. In most cases, we are simply focused on finding you, talking to you about the job opening, doing an initial interview, and then (if all goes well) introducing you to the person who you will end up working for.

That third type of person is known as the hiring manager. "Hiring manager" is just a term we use; that isn't the person's actual title. The hiring manager is the person who will be your supervisor. If you're in sales, this person might be the Director of Sales. If you're in manufacturing, this might be the VP of Manufacturing.

The hiring manager is the person who will make the actual decision about whether to offer you a job. It's her team, after all. We recruiters and HR generalists are simply helping this person to find qualified candidates.

In most companies, it's rare for a hiring manager to be your first contact. Usually the hiring manager prefers that we HR folks conduct initial interviews with people. In tiny companies, however, there may not be a human resources department at all—so your first contact might be directly with your new supervisor.

I highly recommend that you look up your initial contact person on LinkedIn and see who you're dealing with before you talk to her. If you're communicating with an HR professional, you may have a very different conversation than you would with a hiring manager.

Recruiters and HR generalists will have only a basic understanding of the job you applied for. The hiring manager, by contrast, is the expert at the job and knows exactly what she needs. Your conversations with each of us will be different in depth and scope.

If your first contact is with a recruiter or HR generalist, your goal can simply be to come across as friendly, answer any questions, and help us identify the matches between your skills and our job opening. Then we can turn to the hiring manager and say, "Hey, I found a wonderful candidate! He seems like a great guy, and he has these five specific things from the job description."

If you help us find the matches between your background and the job at hand, we will then happily pass your information on to the real decision maker.

The Next Steps

If things go well with the recruiter or HR generalist, then your resume will be sent on to the hiring manager.

This is where your resume receives a *much* deeper read. I myself may not understand the difference between C++14 and C++17 programming languages, but you can bet that the Director of Software understands those differences intimately!

She will likely be reading your resume slowly and carefully in an attempt to determine whether you might be a fit for her job. (This is the point at which *all* the bullets on your resume get read, not just the first one or two.)

Along with your resume, she will have notes from the HR person who just spoke with you. The original conversation you had with us is extremely helpful, as it lets us highlight the matches and give our initial impressions. But it's really up to her to decide whether your background and skills are a good match.

Often there will be some back-and-forth. For example, a hiring manager might say to me, "Dan, can you check with this candidate to make sure that he has used C++17 in an embedded environment? We need that embedded experience." In that case, I'll give you a quick call back and ask you that, along with any other questions.

If the hiring manager is confident that there may be a potential match, she will likely schedule an initial interview with you. This can be a phone interview, a video interview, or an in-person interview.

When you interview with the hiring manager, there are two primary questions that she will be asking herself:

1. Can this candidate help me with my work?
2. Would I enjoy working with this person?

That second question is very important! I cannot state strongly enough how many hiring decisions come down to interpersonal chemistry. Very few managers will hire someone who they feel emotionally disconnected to—regardless of how skilled the person might be.

I have spent countless hours discussing this with my clients. The emotional spark that a hiring manager feels when she talks with you will dominate almost every other element. If the hiring manger says to herself, "I really like this person! He seems like a great guy—friendly, helpful, enthusiastic," that will significantly increase your chances of moving toward an offer.

In order to facilitate the sense of connection, it's best to not blast the hiring manager with an aggressive sales-pitch about your skills. She will certainly ask you about your skills. You will have ample opportunity to answer any questions she has. But that is often secondary to the click of interpersonal chemistry.

Some of my counseling clients stop me at this point and say, "Dan, I'm not schmoozy. I don't know how to spark that chemistry."

I tell them that this spark isn't about charm or charisma. It's about whether you'll be a compatible team member.

Will you work well with others? Will you be helpful and supportive? Will you be able to resolve conflicts? Will you be trustworthy? Those are the things that most hiring managers are looking for—not charisma. A friendly spirit of helpfulness is far more important than charm.

If the initial interview with the hiring manager goes well, you may be invited back to meet several other people you'll be working with. These might be fellow team members, other managers, or (if you're a manager yourself) the people who will be reporting to you.

In this next round of interviews, all the things I mentioned are applicable. Each of the people you meet will be asking themselves, "Is this someone I would enjoy working with? Does he seem friendly and kind? Does he have the ability to help our team with his skills?"

In most companies, three rounds of interviews is usually the maximum. You might have an interview with a recruiter or HR generalist, then an interview with a hiring manager, and finally an interview with the rest of the team. Once you're at that third stage, you can generally assume that you're one of a few final candidates.

Having said that, each organization is unique. Some big tech companies and investment banks conduct as many as *seven* rounds of interviews, complete with flying candidates across the country multiple times. Other companies conduct group interviews at the first or second stage, in which you meet with several interviewers at the same time. There is no set formula.

No matter what the format is for the interviews, people will be assessing your skill-fit for the job, and also assessing whether they feel enthusiastic about the prospect of working with you.

If you keep your focus on being kind and helpful, you'll very likely make a very positive impression on the people you interview with. Developing this sense of interpersonal connection is more important than impressing them with your background.

Flipping the Script in Interviews

Let me revisit a theme that I introduced earlier. You may remember that I wrote about "flipping the script" in the job search chapter. I described shifting from a focus on *getting* a job to a focus on *giving* your gifts.

The same flip can help a great deal during interviews.

I encourage you to flip the script during the interview process, and shift from trying to *get* your interviewer's approval to simply *giving* helpfulness in an enthusiastic way. This can reduce a sense of anxiety and pressure. It can also simultaneously increase that interpersonal chemistry I referenced above.

Paradoxically, the less you focus on trying to impress your interviewer—and the more you simply focus on your desire to help her—the more likely you are to make a positive impression!

I've interviewed a number of candidates over the years who said something like, "Dan, I'd be delighted to help your company in this role. I believe I can be a great contributor. But if it turns out that I'm not the best fit, I'd be happy to recommend a few other people I know. I'd like to help you either way."

What a great statement! That approach is just bursting with helpfulness. Look at the language: "delighted to help," "be a great contributor," "happy to recommend a few other people," "help you either way."

As you can imagine, those people jump to the top of my list. They're not trying to impress me and sell me on themselves. They're simply trying to be helpful. Their helpfulness impresses me more than any sales-pitch they can make.

You too can flip the script, and approach every interview with a spirit of helpfulness. This will make a great impression. Even if you're not the ideal fit for this specific job, your interviewer will likely remember you. She may end up contacting you for an even better-fit position down the road.

Interviews are all about relationship building. Interviewers are looking for people whom they feel comfortable with—people they can trust to help them. Friendliness, helpfulness, enthusiasm, and authenticity go a very long way.

Forming Rapport

Let me go a bit deeper into the relationship-building process. Forming a sense of connection and rapport between yourself and your interviewer is one of the most crucial parts of the process.

As I mentioned, most hiring managers will make their ultimate hiring decisions based on how they *feel*. They might not be aware of this. They might even deny it, and swear that they're simply deciding based on "facts." But almost all decisions are heavily influenced by feelings.

Because of this, *the most important thing you can do in an interview is to help the interviewer feel connected to you.* This supersedes almost everything else.

Now, to be clear: I am not suggesting that you should try to manipulate your interviewer's emotions in order to "sell" them on yourself. Most people will see through manipulative tricks. That is why many people hate sales—they have had negative experiences with emotionally manipulative sales people, and know how uncomfortable that feels.

I am not recommending that you use anything I have shared in a manipulative way. Instead, I recommend that you simply focus on developing a connection with your interviewer. The goal is to help her see you as a trustworthy team member.

In order to develop rapport, let me suggest a basic approach that I share not only with my career counseling clients, but also with my clients who are in the process of dating. (After all, first dates are similar to job interviews!)

The basic rapport-building approach I recommend involves three phases that create a cycle:

1. Point out commonalities between yourself and your interviewer.
2. Share relevant information about yourself.
3. Ask questions of her.

Many interviewers will begin by seeing you in a neutral way. The goal is to help your interviewer move from this neutral place to seeing you as a potential member of her team—her "community." That is why we start by finding commonalities.

When I am contacting candidates for open positions, I usually begin by doing a little research. I try to find one or two things I have in common with the person—even if they seem like silly little things. Then I lead off the conversation with those commonalities.

For example, I have had hundreds of conversations that started like this:

"Cole," I say, "thanks for chatting with me. By the way, I see that you worked for GE Capital in Connecticut. I used to live up on High Ridge Road in Stamford myself."

"Really? You're kidding! I lived next door in New Canaan," Cole says.

"Oh, there was a great sushi place in New Canaan with a little fish pond in the floor. We used to go there all the time. What was that called?"

The conversation goes on from there. But we now see each other as part of a community—the "used-to-live-in-Connecticut" community. This can be a great rapport-builder, even though it seems like a small connection.

Here's another example:

"Josephine," I say, "I appreciate you taking my call. By the way, did I see on LinkedIn that you did some volunteer work with a non-profit that helps coffee-growing communities?"

"Yes, I did. I helped them with some of their fundraising activities."

"What a small world," I say. "When I was in college, I helped a non-profit called Coffee Kids in Providence. I developed their newsletter and even wrote fundraising ads for them. They supported families of coffee growers around the world. I'm delighted to see that there are other non-profits doing that type of work."

And we go on from there. Josephine and I have now established a connection. We're in a "help-coffee-related-non-profits" community.

You would probably laugh if you knew how far I stretch at times for some of these connections. But even the stretch ones can have a powerful rapport-building impact.

Let me borrow a page from the world of social psychology. Our minds are often primed to sort the world into "insiders" and "outsiders." Most people default to seeing everyone they don't know as an outsider. But it feels uncomfortable to be surrounded by outsiders—and so, the mind is constantly seeking for confirmation that the person in front of you is a safe insider.

Finding little commonalities can calm the scanning-for-outsiders part of the mind. It can trigger an "all clear—he's one of us" message. That is a fundamental part of rapport-building. I highly recommend that you look for commonalities as you go through the interview process.

These commonalities don't need to be shared experiences like the ones I named above. They can be shared *values*. For example, you might say:

"I appreciate your commitment to helping your customers have a positive experience. That's my primary goal at work as well. I'm so glad to hear that we share that in common."

"Thanks for letting me know that quality control is so essential to you. I also value that enormously. In fact, I wouldn't want to work for a company that didn't value quality."

"I love your mission of bringing affordable health care to the public. That is a core value of mine as well. It's something I've valued for my entire career."

These type of statements show that you and your interviewer have a shared set of values. Articulating these commonalities will go a long way toward developing a sense of connection.

Sharing Information and Asking Questions

Let me now discuss the next two phases of the rapport-building cycle: sharing relevant information about yourself, and asking questions of your interviewer.

In personal conversations, it's common to gravitate toward a 50/50 balance between talking and listening. You share some thoughts with your friend. Then you ask your friend a question, and let him share his thoughts. A 50/50 split of talking and listening usually makes for a comfortable, well-balanced conversation.

However, in job interviews, there will be more of a focus on you. A common time-split in a job interview is 75/25. You will likely spend around 75% of the conversation sharing about your past work experiences, your skills, and your goals.

Anything more than 75% can start to feel unbalanced. It's best to keep an exchange flowing, as most people find one-sided conversations to be draining. It can be helpful to allow your interviewer to "have the floor" at least 25% of the time.

Some interviewers will be naturally chatty. (Especially those of us who do recruiting!) These people may naturally pull you toward a balance during the interview.

For less chatty interviewers, you may want to sprinkle in questions throughout your interview. Questions allow you to take a break from sharing about yourself, and give your interviewer room to talk.

As an example, candidates have asked me things like:

"How would you describe the culture of your company?"

"What type of personality does the hiring manager have? What is her style?"

"Can you describe the growth trajectory for the company? What is the goal over the next couple of years?"

INTERVIEWS

And people also ask me questions about myself:

"Dan, what's your favorite part of recruiting for this company?"

"Do you only focus on executive searches?"

"I see that you have a Colorado phone number. Where do you live?"

I get that last question all the time, and it's a great bridge to a new commonality-finder. When I tell candidates that I live in Boulder, some say:

"You live in Boulder? Oh, I love Boulder. I once stopped by there on a cross-country trip. We went to Rocky Mountain Park and saw all the elk on the roads. You must love living out there. What brought you to Colorado?"

Now, that's a fun topic for me. Forget about the job for a minute—let's talk about Colorado! If we spend five or ten minutes comparing notes about Boulder, we'll move on in the interview with a deeper sense of connection.

You'll have to get a "read" on your interviewer, of course. But in general, it's perfectly fine—and often ideal—to ask your interviewer questions. You can do this to gather information about the job opportunity and company. You can also ask questions to develop the bond between you and the other person.

The Four Common Questions

Let's now discuss a few questions that an interviewer might ask you. Again, it's likely that up to 75% of the time in an interview, you'll be answering questions and talking about yourself.

There are endless questions that you might be asked. If you search online, you can find lists of hundreds of potential questions—including the old-fashioned, "Where do you see yourself in five years?" (I personally don't know anyone who has ever asked this.)

You're welcome to look through those lists of questions and think about them. However, there are four questions in particular that I recommend you prepare answers for in advance.

These four questions are as follows:

1. What interests you about this particular job?
2. Why are you seeking a new position?
3. Can you tell me about a successful work experience, and what it showed?
4. Can you tell me about a difficult work experience, and what you learned?

Now, an interviewer may not use that exact language. But it's very common to receive variations of those four questions. I'll cover some specific variants below.

As a reminder, let me reiterate something I mentioned at the beginning of this book. One of the top "interview techniques" I recommend is to use *stories* when you answer questions.

Stories and anecdotes will illustrate your points more skillfully than any other method of communication. Stories will help the interviewer understand details of your experiences in a very personal way.

As an example of this, let's pretend that I am interviewing for a recruiting role with a corporate client. The CEO of the company says, "Dan, tell me why you'd like to help us with recruiting."

If I were to give a standard answer, I might say, "I've been working as a recruiter for over twenty years. I've completed searches for C-level executives, engineers, sales people, and technical production workers. I feel confident about my ability to fill your searches, and I'd love to help your company."

Now, that's an OK answer. It's an accurate description of my work. There's nothing wrong with it.

However, if I use a *story* to answer that question, the impact will be greater and more personal. Here's how it might look:

The CEO of the company says, "Dan, tell me why you'd like to help us with recruiting."

I say, "You know, I was 27 years old when I did my first recruiting search. It was the dot-com era, and I had to find a Perl programmer for a company in Brooklyn. Do you know Perl? It's this old-school programming language that looks like spaghetti with lines and dashes. The language was old-fashioned even back then, and people were tough to find. I searched for Perl programmers for weeks. When I finally found a great candidate, I felt like a dog who had found a buried bone. It was such a blast to help the company find a programmer, and also help that Perl coder find a home. After twenty years, I'm still like that dog looking for bones. I love the hunt, and I love to build teams."

The CEO might be smiling at that story. If she wants more detail, I'll give her another story, and another. I'll let my stories do the talking. They will illustrate my actual work experience far better than any rote description.

You don't need to come up with a large number of stories. Just a few are fine. Also, your stories don't have to be incredibly interesting or funny. Just a quick anecdote like I gave above is great. If you have a few stories in your pocket—especially for the "successful work experience" and "difficult work experience" questions, it will give you something helpful to draw on.

Let's go through each of the four questions from above. I'll give a few examples of how stories can help with these questions.

The First Question

The first question is an important one: "What interests you about our job?"

It's best if you have a very specific, enthusiastic answer for this one. Even if you're *not* enthusiastic about the entire job, you can nonetheless find a few elements that seem interesting to you. You can focus your answer on these.

While you're preparing an answer for this question, feel free to look through the company's website. Read about their products and services. Learn what their mission is. Study a bit of their history. You can then custom-tailor your response by including some of this information.

Let's imagine that I'm interviewing a job applicant who did a good job researching information before talking to me. She says, "Dan, your company really caught my eye. I saw that you have a number of government contracts in process—including that one with the FDA. I'd love to hear more about that. It would be really exciting to help advance medical technology like you are doing."

Do you know how many people reference this basic level of company detail in interviews with me?

Less than half.

Many job applicants I talk to haven't even taken time to read the website of the company when they talk to me. Some aren't even sure what the company does!

That doesn't upset me personally, but it does lead me to question how excited the person is about this particular job. And I've had hiring managers rule out candidates completely because the candidates didn't take five minutes to learn a bit about the company before an interview.

So it's best to personalize your response to the "What interests you about our job?" question with specific information. You can also weave in a story at this point.

The applicant above might say, "I actually worked on an FDA contract at my last job. It was far more difficult than we thought. Mid-way through the process, our contact at the FDA called us down to Washington and said..."

And so forth. As I mentioned, your stories don't need to be funny or fascinating. But if they're relevant to the matches between your background and the job opening, they will carry a lot of weight.

Your stories illustrate that you've actually *done* the type of work involved in this job. They paint a picture better than any basic description can.

The Second Question

Let's move on to the second question: "Why are you seeking a new position?"

This is a common question. After all, a hiring manager will want to know if you're bored at your current job, or if you are seeking more responsibilities, or if you're underpaid, or if you were recently laid-off.

You can be as disclosing in your answer as you wish. That choice is up to you. If you choose to be open and honest, please make sure that you don't say anything negative about your current or past employers—even if your past experiences were painful. Critical comments in interviews are never received well.

If you'd like to give a less-disclosing, general answer, you can always say, "At this point, I'm looking for new challenges, and your role looks like a great fit."

If you're bored at your current job, you can say that you're looking for new challenges.

If you're underpaid, you can say you're looking for new challenges.

If you were laid-off—well, now you are looking for new challenges!

I receive this "looking for new challenges" answer more than half of the time. It's a fine answer. You can make it even better by adding a story.

For example: "I'm looking for new challenges, and your company seems like a great place to grow. At my past job, I helped build the supply chain group from scratch. We really didn't have any systems in place. It was rewarding to plant seeds and watch them blossom. I'd love to help a company like yours grow your supply chain group as well."

That's a small, simple story—but it gives color. It also gives your interviewer an opening to ask further questions. "Wow, that's great. What were some of the things that you focused on when you were building the supply chain group?" The story can emerge in greater detail from there.

Even if you were laid-off or quit your previous job, you can give an anecdote or two about the great work that you did—and the new challenges you'd like to tackle.

It's very possible that the interviewer won't delve further into questions about why you're seeking a new role. You're off to the races with a discussion of interesting stories and projects.

Third and Fourth Questions

The third and fourth questions—"successful" and "difficult" work experiences—can be handled very skillfully with stories. I always recommend that you have a couple of success stories lined up, plus a couple of stories about a difficult situation that *you learned a lesson from.*

There are many forms that these questions can take. An interviewer might ask you:

"What was your greatest accomplishment at your last job?"
(You can share your success story.)

"Can you tell me a time that you had a conflict with a coworker?"
(You can share your learned-a-lesson story.)

"Is there an example of how you successfully handled a tough project at work?"
(You can share your success story.)

"How have you dealt with angry customers?"
(You can share your learned-a-lesson story.)

"What would you consider to be your top strength?"
(You can share your success story.)

"What is your greatest weakness?"
(You can share your learned-a-lesson story.)

Note that we're going to answer that dreaded "greatest weakness" question with a story. We're not going to share a negative story, but a story about *learning from a difficult challenge.*

By taking this approach, your "greatest weakness" answer becomes a story of personal development and growth. You flipped that question by giving a positive story about how you developed wisdom!

As an example, if a corporate client asked me, "Dan, what is your greatest weakness?" I might pull out one of my learned-a-lesson stories. I'd say:

"I've always had a tendency to defer to hiring managers even if they seemed to be on a wrong track. Let me give an example. I once worked with a manager who gave me an extremely narrow set of parameters. He wanted candidates to be from one of four companies on the other side of the country. I spent months reaching out to hundreds of people at those companies without success. Finally I pushed back and insisted that we open up the parameters. Once we expanded the search, I was able to find a couple of good local candidates quickly. I still do have a tendency to overly defer to hiring managers. However, I'm working on respectfully but firmly stating any disagreements up front."

You can see how that story adds color, and answers the "weakness" question with a learning experience. I may still have a tendency to defer to hiring managers more than I should. However, I'm working on being more outspoken so that we can all benefit. It's a good answer to that question.

Now, is that really my "greatest weakness" in life? Certainly not! Not even close.

I would give a completely different answer to a close friend or family member, or a therapist. But an interviewer isn't acting as a therapist, and interviewers are not looking for our deepest vulnerabilities. Instead, they're looking for self-awareness about an area of growth, and they want to know how we're working with that dynamic.

If you have a story or two of a great accomplishment, and then another story or two about a challenging situation that you successfully learned from, it will make it a lot easier to answer these types of questions.

I recommend to all my counseling clients that they have a handful of these stories in their back pocket.

Freeing the Mind

Let me now share some ideas about the aspect of interviewing that is the most difficult for many people: the anxiety that arises during the process.

Interviewing can be nerve-wracking, especially for people who don't like to be in the spotlight. Many people feel as though they are on stage during an interview. Butterflies, stage fright, and even outright panic can ensue.

This is normal. I myself have become tongue-tied and frozen in interviews, and so have many people I know—even people who don't consider themselves shy or anxious by nature. If you experience these feelings, you are not alone. There's nothing wrong with you. You are not any different than the rest of us.

I share this because one of the best ways to move through the stress of an interview process is to *not fight your feelings*. The "fight/flight/freeze" stress circuits tend to get ramped-up in interviews. If you fight your stress feelings, you will simply end up increasing them.

Instead of resisting your feelings, I recommend that you adopt a radically self-accepting mindset—as best as you can—and hold to it throughout the interview process.

No matter what happens, your fundamental goal will be to practice self-acceptance.

If you lose your train of thought in an interview?
Practice self-acceptance.
If you freeze up and can't get words out?
Practice self-acceptance.
If you are shaking with adrenaline?
Practice self-acceptance.
If you give the "wrong" answer to a question?
Practice self-acceptance.
If you "blow" the interview completely?
Practice self-acceptance.

I encourage you to become a self-acceptance-generating machine. The more self-acceptance you can practice, the clearer your mind will become. This will improve your chances of connecting with your interviewer, and increase the likelihood of a job offer.

Even if the practice of self-acceptance doesn't lead to a job offer, it will make the interview process easier. And that is a reward in and of itself.

If you can develop a pattern of interviewing in a peaceful, self-accepting state of mind, you have accomplished something wonderful that will assist you with future interviews. Any step toward self-acceptance is helpful.

The TEA Cycle

As support for this process, let me return to the TEA Cycle that I mentioned in the job search chapter.

As you may remember, TEA stands for Thoughts—Emotions—Actions. These three elements tend to cycle on each other.

For many people the TEA Cycle in an interview looks something like this:

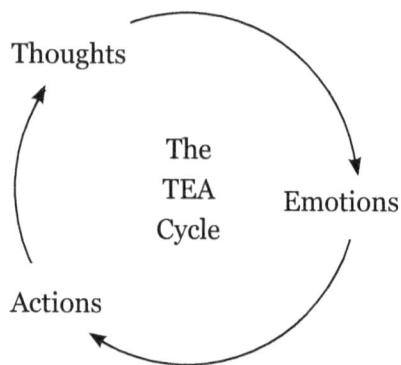

<u>Thoughts</u>:
"I have to impress this person!"
"I need to get this job!"
"I don't think I'm coming across well."
"I have to try harder to make a good impression!"

<u>Emotions</u>:
Self-Pressure
Anxiety
Worry
Self-Consciousness

<u>Actions</u>:
Scramble to come up with impressive things to share.
Try hard to not say the "wrong thing."

INTERVIEWS

Try to figure out what the interviewer wants to hear.
Analyze and monitor how you seem to be "coming across."

All that is completely normal. It is an extremely common TEA Cycle for people who are being interviewed.

But it is an exhausting, draining experience. Mapped out like that, you can see how much pressure, anxiety, and effort this person's mind is putting forth. Even if the interview leads to a job offer, this person may say to himself, "That was awful. I hope I never have to interview for a job ever again."

Let me share an alternate TEA Cycle that you can begin to practice. I will start with self-accepting thoughts, which I mentioned above.

A new TEA Cycle—which will probably take *repeated practice to develop*—might look like this:

Thoughts:
"It's OK if I don't get a job offer. This is good practice."
"It's OK to feel nervous. That's normal."
"It's OK if I don't end up impressing this person."
"I can focus on being helpful and let the chips fall as they will."

Emotions:
Patience with self.
Nervousness *but without fighting it*.
Appreciation for self.
A sense of willingness to go through the process.

Actions:
Focus on commonalities with the interviewer.
Answer and ask questions to develop a connection.
State my enthusiasm about helping the company.
Allow feelings to pass through my awareness
without fighting them.

You can see that the new TEA Cycle starts with a number of self-accepting thoughts. Those thoughts will lay the groundwork for new emotions and actions to blossom.

Instead of walking in with a barrage of self-pressuring, anxiety-producing thoughts, you're deciding right up front that it's OK to not get this job, it's OK to feel nervous, and it's OK to not end up impressing this person. That reduces pressure and anxiety.

"But Dan," some of my clients say at this point, "I *do* need this job!"

I say to them, "You need oxygen, food, and water. But you don't need this job. You might *want* this job, and we'll do everything we can do to increase the odds that there will be a match. But you don't need it. If you insist that you do, you will be flooded with a sense of pressure and anxiety."

The mind responds to the thoughts, "I need oxygen!" and "I need this job!" in a similar way. If you generate those thoughts, the mind will treat both of those as life-or-death scenarios—and it will ramp up every adrenaline and stress circuit at its disposal to keep you alive.

That's great when it comes to oxygen. It's not great when it comes to job interviews.

So it's best to ease off this type of thinking, and instead let the mind know that it's OK to not end up with a job offer. We'll *aim* to get the job; we'll use the methods that I'm covering in this book. But if an offer doesn't come, that's OK. There are plenty of other companies to help.

In the new TEA Cycle, you begin by generating self-accepting, de-pressuring thoughts. You allow nervousness and anxiety to be present without fighting them. You meet those feelings with a sense of patience and appreciation for your efforts to simply show up. You allow your feelings to be present, and give them permission to pass through you like a wave.

INTERVIEWS

You then focus your actions on finding connections and commonalities with your interviewer. You express your desire to be helpful, and your enthusiasm to contribute to the company's goals. You come across as friendly, and highlight matches between the job and your background. Then you practice letting go of results and move on to offer help to another company.

If a job offer comes, that's fantastic. If one doesn't come, that's fine—perhaps there simply wasn't a tight-enough fit. You weren't rejected. You didn't fail. In fact, you may have succeeded in connecting with your interviewer, and she may call you in the future with another job opportunity that's an even better fit.

The more you can practice this new type of TEA Cycle (and it *does* take practice) the easier the interview process will be. I have known people who needed to interview with five, six, or seven different companies before this new TEA Cycle began to solidify. Each time there was more peace and less pressure.

I'll discuss a few more emotional aspects of the interview process in the Q&As that follow. However, let me conclude this section by saying once again that anxiety in the interview process is normal. You can practice meeting anxiety with self-acceptance. You can focus on simply coming across as friendly, and helping your interviewer to understand how you can help her company.

If you do that, you've succeeded—regardless of whether you receive a job offer in the end. At the very least, you have begun to establish a new pattern that will aid you in future interviews with other companies. Every step in the right direction is worth the practice.

After the Interview

After the interview, I recommend that you email a friendly note to each of your interviewers. You can thank them for their time, express your enthusiasm for the position, and state a few things you appreciate about the company.

Do you know how many people send me a note like that after I conduct an interview with them?

Less than 10%.

Candidates probably send notes more frequently to the hiring manager than to me. But my guess is that fewer than 30% of people send thank you notes to anyone.

It's not a requirement to send follow-up notes, of course. But it gives a wonderful boost to your candidacy. At the very least, it demonstrates your thoughtfulness and continued interest in the position. That goes a long way.

Many times, companies will end an interview process with a "tie" between two people. One person may be a slightly better match, but often they're fairly close.

If the first person follows up by expressing their excitement about the position, and the second person goes silent in the days after the interview, it begins to tip the scales *very strongly*.

Every company wants to hire employees who are excited about working there. Some companies even wait a while to see how candidates will respond post-interview. They want to ascertain how enthusiastic the candidates actually are.

So follow-up notes are powerful. You can also reach out by phone to the recruiter or HR generalist you original spoke to, and express your enthusiasm and interest. We may not have a decision yet, but we'll appreciate that you're eager to move forward.

The Decision

Once the company makes a decision about their top choice, one of three things will usually happen:

1. The company will make you a job offer.
2. Or the company will tell you that they decided to make an offer to someone else.
3. Or you will be left in limbo for a while.

As frustrating as it is to be left in limbo—and it *is* frustrating—the limbo scenario isn't always a bad thing. There might be some behind-the-scenes dynamics taking place.

Let's imagine that you are one of the final two candidates for a job opening. The company decides to make an offer to the other candidate. However, they also like you—and would be delighted to have you on their team.

In that scenario, the company will likely extend an offer to the other person, and leave you in limbo for a while.

Why? Because the first person might not accept the offer. If she declines the offer, then the company will make an offer to you.

This has happened many times in my recruiting work. We may be secretly hoping that the first person will decline, because we actually really liked you. We simply had to make an offer to that person due to her remarkably tight skill-fit with our job opening. Or her salary requirements may have been quite a bit lower than yours.

So we give her a few days to consider the offer, and then if she declines, we make you an offer. You were not our "back-up" exactly; we are actually happy that she turned down the offer. We're excited by the prospect of you joining our team.

Again, I have had this happen numerous times. If a company tells you that they're "in the decision process," you might be in a situation where you and another candidate are both good fits.

As with every other aspect of the process, you can simply express your enthusiasm at this point, ask if there is anything you can do to be helpful (including offering additional information), and then let the decision process unfold.

Responding to an Offer

If the company decides to make you an offer, there is often a negotiation process that begins at that point.

What salary or hourly rate are you seeking? Even if this was discussed previously, it's now time to lock-down the numbers. Will there be a bonus or other "variable" element of the compensation package? What about vacation time? Is there an option to work partly from home?

My recommendation during this negotiation phase is to seek "win-win" solutions. A win-win solution is an arrangement where both you and the company feel happy with the result.

I do *not* recommend that you aggressively push to extract as much as you can from the company, without regard for their happiness. I have seen this approach sour many compensation discussions. You can push, of course—but push for a *win-win solution* where both you and the company feel happy with the arrangement.

I will write more about win-win dynamics in chapter twelve of this book. However, for now, let me share a conversation to illustrate win-win negotiations. This conversation is similar to many that I have had.

"Cassandra," I say, "everyone really enjoyed meeting you. They would love to have you join their team. I'd like to extend an offer to you on behalf of the company. Now, did I remember that you were looking for a salary of around $75,000?"

"That's wonderful to hear!" says Cassandra. "Yes, something around $75,000 would be great. I'm wondering if there might be an opportunity to earn a bonus as well if I were to exceed my goals."

"You know," I say, "we weren't planning to include a bonus for this position. But what were you thinking?"

"I'm flexible—but I know a few people in my type of position who earn a 10% bonus for exceeding goals. Is that something that you might consider?"

"I'm happy to check," I say. "If we can't do a bonus, would a straight salary of $80,000 feel comfortable for now?"

"Sure, that would be great," says Cassandra. "However, could you check to see if the company might be open to including a bonus in the future? Perhaps in my second year, if I'm meeting all my goals? I really love to have something to stretch for."

And the conversation goes on from there. You can see that Cassandra is skillfully presenting options and requests, while keeping things positive and friendly. She's making it very easy for me to work with her.

If I can convince the higher-ups, I might be able to come back to her with an offer for $80,000 and a commitment to set up a bonus program at her one-year anniversary.

In this process, we are seeking win-win solutions together. The tone is friendly and respectful on both sides. This approach is much more successful than pushing to extract concessions until the other side hits a breaking-point.

Again, I will write more about this later, as finding win-win solutions is an art that can help with many aspects of your work life.

For now, I'll suggest that you lead any type of salary negotiations with a statement like, "I'd like to find an arrangement that we both feel good about." That establishes a cooperative playing field. It places you in alignment with the company, rather than at odds.

As a final note: If you are told in the end that the company will *not* be moving forward with an offer to you, please remember that you did not fail. You were not rejected. There simply wasn't a tight-enough match for this role, at this time.

You very generously offered to help the company. You met with people there and formed connections. You accomplished all that you needed to do.

You can now move on to offer help to another company or organization. Acting from this spirit of helpfulness, you will very likely find a number of happy takers for your offering.

CHAPTER NINE

Interviews: A Deeper Look

In the last chapter, we explored the flow of the interview process from your first contact with a company all the way to salary negotiations. As a reminder, coming across as helpful and friendly—and focusing on a connection with your interviewer—is the most important thing you can do.

Let me now take a deeper look at the process of interviewing by sharing some questions I have received.

Q: I recently interviewed with a company and had a great connection with everyone. I was sure I'd get an offer. But to my surprise, they decided to go with a different candidate. What do you think happened?

A: We can never know for sure. But there are three common scenarios that might have occurred.

In the first scenario, everyone at the company may have really enjoyed meeting you. But perhaps there was a candidate who had just a *slightly* tighter skill-fit for the job opening. There's nothing you can do about that, except to keep the door open and the relationship positive.

The other candidate might decide the day before she's scheduled to start that she changed her mind and will not be joining the company. I've had this happen!

Or she may join, and then decide to leave after a few weeks. I've had this happen as well!

Or perhaps in a few months, the company may find that they need a second person to join the team. This happens frequently.

Any number of things may play out. Because of that, it's a good idea to keep the channels of communication open and friendly while you pursue new opportunities.

As a second scenario, the company may have promoted someone from within to fill the role. Some companies have a pre-selected person that they want to promote into an opening, but due to company policy they are required to conduct a public recruiting search.

I disagree with policies like this. They are designed to minimize favoritism and keep the playing field open, but they usually end up wasting people's time and creating false hope for outside candidates. In every situation I recall, the company went with their "inside" person despite interviewing multiple "outside" candidates. Thankfully, this isn't very common.

A third possibility is that the company experienced a change in business conditions mid-way through the interview process. Perhaps they just learned that they are going to merge with a larger company, and that all hiring is temporarily frozen. Or perhaps a big sale was delayed. The company won't disclose this to you—they will simply say that you were not selected for the position.

This type of situation happens very frequently. As with the other two scenarios, there's really nothing you can do about this development except to keep the communication channel open and positive.

Perhaps after the company completes its merger, or the sale comes in, they will contact you and see if you might still be interested—especially if things stay friendly and open between you.

In all of these scenarios, the people you interviewed with may have really liked you. They may truly want to have you join them.

INTERVIEWS Q&A

I recommend that you keep an open and positive connection with them, as conditions may change at any point.

Q: I keep interviewing over and over without getting an offer, and I have no idea what I'm doing wrong. I ask for feedback, but no one wants to be honest with me. Is there anything I can do?

A: It's unlikely that a recruiter or hiring manager will give you honest feedback about how your interview went. You can certainly ask, but it's rare for companies to be disclosing about why they chose another candidate.

If this is a pattern, I recommend scheduling a session with a career counselor. You can then run through some "mock" interviews in order to receive feedback. I have done this with many clients, and in almost all cases there are blind spots in communication styles that need to be identified and changed.

For example, some people give such complex, lengthy answers to interview questions that the interviewer becomes bored and disinterested. I've had hiring managers say, "Dan, I couldn't even get a word in with that candidate!"

Other people do the opposite; they give extremely curt, sparse answers. The interviewers are forced to ask follow-up question after follow-up question in order to "pull out" information. This also diminishes the interpersonal connection that we're aiming for.

Running through a practice interview with a career counselor—or a trusted friend or family member—can provide some feedback about these types of dynamics. You can even take a step further, and record a video of the practice interview in order to review the flow of communication.

As I mentioned, establishing a connection with your interviewer is key. If you're forming connections, you're probably on a good track. You might simply need to keep plugging along.

If you *aren't* feeling a strong connection with your interviewers, there may be a number of communication style shifts that will help.

Q: Should I bring copies of my resume to an interview? Or anything else?

A: Sure, it's a good idea to bring a few copies of your resume. Some of your interviewers might not have a copy in front of them. Your resume gives them a great jumping-off point to ask specific questions about your experience.

Just make sure to bring the same version of your resume that you originally submitted to the company. As you remember, I recommend that you slightly edit the "summary" section and the first few bullets of your recent jobs in order to highlight matches. Please double-check that you're bringing the correct version.

For added impact, you can also bring additional materials to share with your interviewer. These might be samples of your work, a reference letter, or even an outline of some initiatives that you can help the company with.

Let me share a quick story about this. I once worked for a company that interviewed a candidate to be their CEO. Prior to his interview, the candidate hired a private librarian to track down the company's international shipments—information that was not easily available. He brought a copy of the shipping report to the interview.

What an impact that document made! The company owners were fascinated that he had been able to identify that information. It impressed them about his ability to pull together data. It also gave them something to talk about in the interview. I remember them flipping through the report long after he left.

If there is something helpful and relevant that you can leave with your interviewers, it can have a nice impact.

Q: When a company asks me about my salary, do I have to tell them? I'm underpaid right now and would prefer not to discuss it.

A: "What is your current salary?" used to be a standard question in interviews. However, an increasing number of cities and states are banning that question completely, in order to reduce pay disparities and inequity. So you will probably be asked this less frequently as time goes on.

I myself always ask candidates, "Can you tell me what salary/wage you're *looking for* in a new role?" Most recruiters these days will only ask about your salary desires. We will not ask about your history.

If you are asked about your current compensation, and you don't feel comfortable sharing details, you might try redirecting the question by stating your goals. Here's how that would look:

A recruiter asks, "Can I ask what you're currently making?"

You say, "Well, I'm ideally looking for $50,000 for a new position."

You simply bridge to your new target. Many recruiters will be OK with that answer, and won't press you about your current salary or wage. You've just told them the most important thing.

If they do ask again, you can say, "Honestly, I'm being paid less than market rate in my current job, but I'd really like to get up to $50,000 in a new job."

Another option is to visit Salary.com or another salary survey site, and say, "I've done some research on salaries for this type of position, and it seems as though the median is $50,000. Is that in the range of what you'd be comfortable with?"

Recruiters are generally looking for a ballpark number in order to ensure that you're in the same range as other candidates. They don't usually care about tracking your salary history.

Although it's rare, you might be asked about your current salary on an application form, rather than in an interview. It's up to you about whether to leave that part of the form blank. (You can always write, "Will discuss in person," or something similar.)

If you're *required* to disclose your salary history on an ATS form, I don't recommend that you lie. Instead, share the information and then explain to the company in an interview that you have been paid "under market" and that you're seeking $50,000.

You can also share a story about why you stayed at a below-market rate job. Perhaps you loved the company, the people, and the work. You can turn your under-market pay history into a testament about your loyalty.

But then let them know what salary or wage you're seeking in a new job. That is what really matters.

Q: I have a criminal conviction on my record, and I don't know whether to disclose that in an interview. Do you have any thoughts?

A: I have worked with a large number of counseling clients with a variety of criminal convictions, including felonies and sex offenses. So I am very sensitive to how challenging the job search process can be when criminal history is involved.

You'll have to make your own decisions about this. However, you should be aware that an increasing number of states and municipalities have "ban the box" laws which prevent companies from asking about criminal history at early stages of the application process.

Because of that, most of us in the HR world do not ask about criminal history. We usually *do* run a criminal background check as part of the job offer process. But if that background check comes back "clean," we don't dig around for information. We allow the background check service to do the investigating.

You should consult with your attorney and ask her about how your record may appear. I would defer to your attorney's opinion on how to proceed. However, I can say that many criminal records are either sealed, or have expired within a particular locality's reporting timeframe, and therefore do not show up on criminal background checks. Therefore, you might sidestep the entire issue.

If there is a criminal event that you're certain will show up on a background check—and you're fairly sure that the company will run a check—then you might consider discussing your situation in an interview. I have had candidates disclose their experiences in the initial interviews with me, and I certainly appreciated their honesty. Each company will have a its own level of comfort with conviction histories.

While we're on the topic, let me share a strategy that I have recommended to some of my counseling clients. If you have a felony-level conviction in your background, and are struggling to find a company that will hire you, you might want to consider self-employment—or pursuing a line of work that allows you to set yourself up as an independent contractor.

For example, let's say that you set up a landscaping business and then approach corporations about providing landscaping for their office complexes. If they hire your *company*, they will very likely not request any type of background check on you. After all, you're a business that they are working with. You are not an employee of theirs.

People who work on an independent contractor basis—whether they are website developers, office cleaners, drywall repairers, lead generators, or anything else—are often not background-checked. I have had numerous counseling clients who successfully went down the freelance, independent contractor, or self-employment route due to criminal backgrounds.

And of course, there are corporations that are open to hiring people with felony backgrounds. Some of these companies were founded by people with felony histories themselves, and they are committed to giving folks another chance. Feel free to do some research online as the list of companies is frequently changing.

Q: *I interviewed with a company last year, and never received any further contact after the interview. I assume that they filled the position, but I have no idea. Why do companies sometimes stop communicating like that?*

A: Ideally, that should never happen. On behalf of all of us in the recruiting world, I want to apologize. Everyone who interviews deserves clear communication about the final decision on filling a role.

Perhaps the recruiter lost track of whom he had already contacted. I'm sure I've made this mistake myself. Or perhaps the company put the search on hold and hasn't yet made a decision.

If you haven't heard from the company within a few weeks of your interview, please go ahead and reach out to them. You might want to first try the recruiter or HR generalist whom you originally spoke to, but you can also directly contact the hiring manager. They might be able to share an update with you.

If they outright ignore you—well, that's not a company that I personally would want to work for. You may have dodged a bullet.

In my own work, I can't respond to every applicant for a job. But I certainly try to communicate clearly about decisions to anyone who has been through the interview process. Again, our apologies. Hopefully this will not happen to you again.

Q: *A commitment to diversity, equity, inclusion, and accessibility (DEIA) is important to me. Is it OK to ask about policies like these in an interview?*

Sure, it's perfectly appropriate to ask about DEIA initiatives and any other company policies at any stage of your interview. The HR professionals might have the deepest understanding of specific practices (especially as they relate to hiring and professional development), so they might be the best people to ask.

INTERVIEWS Q&A

I do suggest that you take an encouraging approach with your questions. Some smaller companies may not have spent much time thinking about diversity and inclusion efforts. They might not have a policy in place. However, they might be eager to learn about DEIA initiatives.

A direct question like, "What is your DEIA policy?" may be met with confusion at small companies. An alternative might be to say, "I have a commitment to supporting diversity, equity, inclusion, and accessibility in the workplace. Is your company open to efforts to support those?"

Companies who have a DEIA commitment will immediately share the details of their own efforts with you. Companies that *haven't* thought a great deal about diversity and inclusion may nonetheless be delighted to receive your insights about strengthening new practices.

On a related note, you can also ask your interviewers about the broader culture at their company. General questions like, "What is your company culture?" might be challenging for some interviewers to answer. But if you lead with your interests, it will make it easy for the person to respond.

For example, you might say, "I've really enjoyed working with companies that have a team-focused, collaborative culture. Is that part of your company's culture, as you see it?" Most people will respond very positively (and often, very honestly) to questions like these.

Q: Dan, I read your comments about working with anxiety. But I've had full-blown panic attacks in interviews, where I had to leave the room. I'm terrified to interview again and have been avoiding interviews for years. What can I do about that?

A: I am aware of how truly overwhelming panic symptoms can be. You are courageous for wanting to work with this dynamic. Some people simply drop out of the work world entirely after encountering panic-inducing situations in the workplace.

My answer is that I encourage you to schedule a few sessions with a counselor or psychologist who specializes in working with panic symptoms. You deserve direct, personalized support.

Having said that, let me outline a few approaches from the world of cognitive behavioral therapy that you can discuss further with a therapist.

You might find it helpful to practice replacing old self-pressuring thought patterns with new de-pressuring, self-accepting thoughts. The key is to begin to strengthen these new thought patterns *well before your interview takes place.*

I often tell my clients that the process is like going to the gym. If you have to lift something very heavy in a month, you don't want to wait until that day and try to "ramp up" your strength.

Instead, it's best to go to the gym today, and lift a few weights gently. Then go again in another day or two and lift some more. Then again. After a few weeks of this, you will be significantly stronger. So it is with the mind as well.

You can begin today to strengthen a new de-pressuring, self-accepting thought pattern that says something like this:

"It's OK to feel panicked in an interview. It's just my adrenaline and stress circuits firing. Many people feel that way. If I have to leave an interview because I'm feeling overwhelmed, that's OK. There are plenty of other companies to interview with. If I feel panicked, it doesn't mean that I've done anything wrong. It doesn't mean that I'm flawed. It just means that this area of life is challenging for me, just as it is for many other people."

The goal is to strengthen that new way of thinking in a calm, gradual way over time. As you practice thinking that way on a day-to-day basis, you might eventually find that those thoughts form a general "attitude" that runs on its own in the background. That is the goal.

You might also talk to a therapist about the process of "graduated exposure." I strongly recommend that people work with a therapist on this type of approach, rather than go it alone.

The process of graduated exposure involves *gently, gradually,* and *repeatedly* entering into situations that trigger a small, manageable amount of anxiety. Over time, you gently increase your depth.

As an example, you might take five minutes to sit down with a friend (or even your pet!) and pretend that you're answering one interview question.

Just one interview question. Perhaps with your sweet cat.

You do that every night for a week.

Once that becomes easy, you increase to several questions in a row.

Then 15 or 20 minutes of questions.

Then you record a video of that interview practice and review the video by yourself.

Then you review the video with another person and invite feedback.

And so forth. The goal is to help the mind develop a greater comfort with the interview process through *gentle, gradual* repeated steps. Eventually, you might apply for a job that you're not really interested in, simply to practice interviewing in a low-stakes environment.

Again, I recommend that you do not do this without help from a therapist. People have a tendency to overshoot in this process, get overwhelmed, and stop the process entirely. A good counselor or therapist can help you pace the steps in a gentle, gradual manner.

On the mindfulness level, you can practice what I call the "waves" technique: You can give your feelings permission to arise in your awareness, and then pass through you, as if you were standing waist-deep in the ocean encountering a series of waves.

In this process, you don't battle against your feelings. Instead, you hold your center as you allow the feelings to rise up in your awareness and then pass by.

When the next wave comes, you do the same: Allow it to rise up in your awareness, and then pass by. You don't fight or hide from your feelings. You simply allow them to rise up and pass through you while you hold your center.

A mindfulness-oriented counselor or therapist can help you with this process. If you'd like to research therapists who specialize in these types of techniques, you might want to look up "cognitive behavioral therapy," "dialectical behavioral therapy," or "acceptance and commitment therapy," often referred to as CBT, DBT, or ACT.

There are countless other therapy modalities, of course. Any of them can be helpful. I encourage you to follow your own inner wisdom as you reach out for help. Your courage to tackle this dynamic is admirable, and deserves to be supported.

•

Let me conclude this chapter with a summary of the themes I have covered.

Anxiety is normal in interviews. Anxiety shows that you care about the job, and want to make a good impression. (If you didn't care about your interview, you probably wouldn't feel anything but boredom.)

Most companies are not looking for smooth operators. Instead, they're looking for friendly, trustworthy people who are authentic and kind. You can focus on simply being helpful in your interview. Whether or not you receive a job offer, you will very likely make a positive impression.

The first person you might talk to is a recruiter or human resources generalist. You can focus on relationship-building with these people, and help them to see the "matches" between your skills and the job at hand.

If that goes well, you will likely speak next with the hiring manager. This is the person you will be working for, and she is the real decision-maker.

In your interview with her, you can focus on developing a sense of connection and rapport. She will ask you about your skills and background; you will have plenty of time to describe those. But often, the sense of connection is even more important.

Stories and anecdotes can be a great way to answer questions in an interview. You may want to prepare a few stories in advance, especially stories about positive accomplishments, and stories about challenging experiences that you learned from. You may be asked about "strengths" and "weaknesses"—and if so, you can draw on those stories.

If you receive a job offer, you can aim for win-win solutions when you have discussions about salary.

If you do not receive a job offer, you have not been rejected. You have not failed or done anything wrong. There simply wasn't a match for this role, at this time. You can move on to offer your help to another company.

Let me now discuss a different path through the world of work: self-employment.

CHAPTER TEN

Self-Employment

In my career counseling practice, I've had the pleasure of working with a large number of entrepreneurs. It's always enjoyable to help people launch and grow businesses.

If you're considering self-employment, this chapter will help you begin that process. I'll be sharing ideas about selecting products and services to offer, reaching out to new customers, and the value of specializations.

Let me begin by revisiting what I wrote earlier in this book.

When I have a client who is interested in opening a business, I usually check a few things. I ask her if she will be comfortable engaging in sales, marketing, and other outreach activities. I ask about her tolerance of rise-and-fall income cycles. I ask her what she will do if her business doesn't turn out to be viable.

I also sometimes share a few stories to see how my clients react to various scenarios.

For example, in the first year of my recruiting business, I completed one job with a corporate client and a second job with a fellow recruiter. I sent each of them invoices when my work was done.

When I didn't receive payment after a month, I called to follow-up. Each of them said to me in so many words, "I'm not going to pay you. You can sue me if you like."

What a shock that was!

If an employer decides not to pay you, there are labor laws that will back you up. But if someone decides to not pay your business after you've completed work—well, you're somewhat on your own. You can hire an attorney to do collections, or take other steps, but in business-to-business transactions, labor laws aren't there to protect you.

I share stories like these because it's essential to approach self-employment with wide open eyes. Part of my job as a career counselor is to help clients understand both the benefits and risks of running a business. Self-employment is a journey that will have challenges at times.

Having said that, self-employment can also be enormously rewarding. It can give you skills that you might never have gained in traditional employment. It can help you learn and grow.

In those two non-payment situations above, I ended up negotiating to get paid around half of what I was owed. It took months of back-and-forth conversations, but I found a way to proceed.

That was a valuable learning process. In my mid-twenties, being a sensitive guy with a sheltered work background, I was not prepared to go head-to-head in negotiations over payment for jobs I had completed. But I learned how to do it, and it was a strengthening experience.

In this chapter, I'll share some of the practical steps I discuss with my clients who are considering self-employment. My goal is to help you set the groundwork for a business, even if you have no idea where to begin.

There Is No Failure

One important idea I share with my clients is that *there is never any failure* in the world of self-employment. There is only learning.

The first business you set up may not last forever. It may not make a great deal of money. But that doesn't mean that anything failed. You will still learn an enormous amount from the process of launching a business—knowledge that will remain with you.

Your self-employment experience may turn out to be a stepping stone to a completely different chapter in your career, even if your business doesn't last. Most successful entrepreneurs can share stories of multiple early businesses that didn't work out, but led to later successes.

Let me give an example of this from my own life. Shortly after I graduated from college, I taught myself HTML, the scripting language behind websites. I then set up a website design company and began creating sites for local businesses and non-profits.

My business didn't earn much money. However, I enjoyed it. It felt like the right thing to do at the time.

After a year, a client of mine introduced me to a company in Brooklyn that developed intranet systems for an investment bank.

I had a conversation with the CEO of the intranet company that went like this:

"So Dan," he said, "I looked at your portfolio. It looks like you develop websites in HTML. Is that right?"

"Yes," I said. "I'm wondering if you need help with overflow work."

"We actually use a language called Perl to create our sites. You don't know Perl, do you? We're having trouble finding Perl programmers."

"No, I don't know Perl," I said. "But I've done some recruiting work in the past. Would you like help finding Perl programmers?"

"You can do that? Sure, that would be great. We can't afford typical recruiter fees though."

"How about this," I said. "I'll charge you a third of what many recruiters charge. And you only have to pay me if I find someone you like. Would that work?"

"That works!" he said.

The very next day, I stopped looking for website clients and opened a software recruiting business.

Was my website business a failure? Not at all. It was an interesting experience, and led me to a next step.

Did it make a lot of money? No, but it was still a success as a stepping stone.

In the same way, you might set up a business that leads you to another business, job, or career path. A non-viable business is still a learning experience, and a step to something else.

I encourage all of my clients to make peace in advance with the idea that their first, second, or third business idea might not pan out. Even if that happens, these business ventures will provide valuable lessons.

"But Dan," some people say, "I'm planning to sink my life savings into my business. If I fail, I'll be ruined."

I respect everyone's choices. However, I always encourage people to travel down the self-employment path in a way that is *enjoyable*. Ventures that risk financial ruin are usually extremely stressful, and often end in painful ways.

I have worked with numerous clients who came to me for counseling because they had invested all of their money in an unsuccessful business idea and were now in a state of financial strain. That can be a very difficult emotional experience.

Because of that, I encourage people to proceed along the self-employment path in an enjoyable, peaceful way. It can be done.

There are many people who disagree with my approach. They say, "You only live once! Put it all on the line! Go big or go home!" But I've helped numerous people pick up the pieces after shutting down a business, and I encourage a less stressful approach to self-employment.

Having said that, I do know people who poured everything they had into a venture, and experienced great success. Although I vote for a peaceful approach, I respect everyone's choices.

SELF-EMPLOYMENT

Starting with a Need

Whether you plan to take a gentle-and-gradual or a big-and-bold approach to self-employment, you'll need to choose a product or service to offer.

Let me share some wisdom that I once received on this subject. When I was young, I told my father that I planned to set up a business. I was going to sell something that I was very excited about.

I don't remember the details of my business idea, but I do remember vividly what he said.

"Danny," he told me, "don't set up a business simply because it excites you. Make sure that your business also provides something that people *want* and *need*."

I remember the conversation because I was incredibly disappointed to hear that. It was like a splash of cold water. Who cared what people needed? I wanted to do what was exciting to me!

Over the years, I developed an appreciation for his words. Eventually I realized how very few people approach self-employment in this way, and how many businesses close down because of it.

Many entrepreneurs start with a product that excites them. They set up a business to offer that product. Then, as a final step, they try to find customers.

Although that approach can be successful, I've met many business owners who never found a market for their offering. There simply wasn't a need for their product in the first place.

It can be far more effective to go in the other direction. You can first explore the needs of the people and companies around you. Then you can brainstorm about exciting products to meet those needs. That approach has a far greater success rate, in my experience.

Let me return to my story. Did I start with a vision of recruiting Perl programmers? Not at all. I had never even heard of the language. But right in front of me was a company with a need, and it seemed like a great way help them.

I went on to recruit software developers who used all sorts of strange languages: Fortran, Delphi, MATLAB, and others. I never planned to build a business recruiting those people, but those were the needs that presented at the time. As needs (and programming languages) changed over time, I changed my focus and offerings.

I encourage you to begin by looking around and listening. What are people and companies around you struggling with? What do they need help with? What needs and desires are not being met?

Once you identify several needs, you can come up with wonderful ideas about how to meet those needs. You can choose something that's exciting to you—something you're passionate about. But starting with the assessment of needs can be a helpful first step.

As trends change over time, you can continue to ask: What do the people and companies around me need *now*? Can I help them with their new needs in a way that will be enjoyable?

I have known successful "serial entrepreneurs" who took this approach and created one new business after another to meet changing needs. These entrepreneurs' ability to listen and respond gave birth to numerous great businesses.

Choosing What to Offer

"OK, Dan," you might be thinking, "I know a bunch of needs. I'd love to create a business to meet those needs. But where do I begin?"

To help you answer that question, let me share a three-dimensional model that can help you choose a business offering (or several). This model is designed to creatively stretch your imagination.

For this discussion, I'm going to assume that you're only considering a journey into self-employment, and haven't yet decided what to offer in your business. However, if you already have a business set up, you can still use this model to expand your current offerings.

The first of the three dimensions in the model involves the choice of *services* and *products*.

Some self-employed people offer only services. When you get your taxes done by an accountant, the accountant is providing a service to you. She is spending her time and skill to work on your taxes. She isn't selling you a finished product.

Doctors, landscapers, attorneys, pet sitters, electricians—all these people are offering services. You pay these people for their time to do a specific action. Their services are custom-tailored to your needs.

By contrast, other businesses offer products rather than services. My region in Colorado is known for its specialty foods product companies. We have many small businesses that produce organic salsa, granola, coffee cakes, snack bars, chocolate, and numerous other tasty things. The entrepreneurs who started these companies are offering packaged products—not services.

There are other businesses that create blends of products and services. For example, if you hired someone to design and print business cards for you, that person would be creating a service/product mix: working with you to create a design (service), and then printing up the cards for you to use (product).

When clients of mine are considering self-employment, I encourage them to explore various points within this service/product dimension.

Would you be interested in offering a service? Or a finished product? Or perhaps some type of mix or blend? Try to get a sense of what appeals to you. See what your inner compass pulls you toward.

You may want to consider a mix of offerings as you're starting out. If you're leaning toward a service, is there a product that you can offer as well? If you have a product offering, is there a related service that you can add on? At the early stages of a business, it can be helpful to have a diversity of offerings.

To illustrate this first dimension, here are three examples along the service/product continuum:

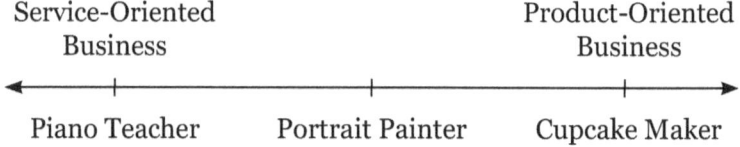

The piano teacher is offering a service. The cupcake maker is creating a finished product. The portrait painter is somewhere in the middle; he provides a service to custom-create a finished product for you.

No matter what need you're planning to help with, you can probably create multiple solutions along this service/product continuum.

Let me return to my Perl programmer story. I provided a service to the company. I helped them actively recruit programmers. I offered my time, effort, and recruiting skill on a per-job basis.

However, I could have offered a *product* instead of a service. For example, I could have set up a "Perl jobs in Brooklyn" website and sold that website to the company. Or I could have written a book called *How to Recruit Perl Programmers* and sold that.

Or I could have offered something blended between product and service: I could have provided recruiting for the company (service), and also created a "Perl recruiting tips" manual (product) for their own HR people to use internally.

If you identify a need, and are interested in creating a solution, you can ask yourself whether a service, a product, or something blended appeals to you.

If you have decided to offer something at one point in that continuum, you can consider a few other offerings at other points. You might be surprised at how many business offerings you can come up with.

Pros and Cons

Before moving on to the second dimension, let me discuss a few pros and cons of service and product businesses.

Service businesses often require very little money to set up. In essence, you are offering your labor; you are not required to manufacture, store, and ship products. You can generally take on assignments as you wish. There is usually a great deal of flexibility.

However, service businesses (especially solo businesses) only run when you do the work. They are often difficult to scale-up in size, and it's sometimes difficult to sell the business if you want to exit the company. After all, your service *is* the business.

Product-oriented businesses, by contrast, often require an initial financial investment. If you are creating a food product, you will need a commercial kitchen and a storage facility. If you're creating clothing, you will need a place to sew and ship the products. If you're manufacturing something, you might need a specially-zoned manufacturing facility.

The benefit of a product-oriented business is that the business can run without your direct involvement—and therefore, can be sold more easily. If your granola product is great, it will be great whether you own the business or someone else does. The value of the business is in the product itself, not the service provider.

Some entrepreneurs like to provide services; others like to offer products. There is no right or wrong decision. As I mentioned, you might be able to fulfill any type of need with a service, a product, or some type of blended offering.

I always encourage my newly-started entrepreneurs to stretch their imagination in their offerings. We never know what will catch on until we begin to offer it. Having multiple products and services can be helpful at the beginning.

The Second Dimension

Let's now move onto the second dimension in the model. The second dimension involves business offerings that are *concrete* versus those in the realm of *ideas*.

Your business can offer concrete, physically-oriented services and products. Or you can offer services and products that are more ideas-based. Let me give a few examples.

Lawn care companies operate in the physical world. A lawn care professional will bring beauty to your property not by sharing ideas about it, but by actively planting, shaping, and modifying things. It is a service business, but a physically-oriented one.

Counseling and therapy businesses, by contrast, operate in the world of ideas. When I conduct a counseling session, I am discussing thoughts and feelings with my clients. The service is a series of conversations. The business is a flow of ideas.

Products can also be either physical or ideas-oriented. Most products are concrete: cars, cookies, treadmills, phones. These products are manufactured, stored, shipped, and eventually consumed, recycled, or thrown out.

Cloud-based software products, by contrast, are far less tangible. The only physical manifestation of a cloud-based product is digital code stored on a distant server, with output loaded onto your screen. There is no "thing" to be manufactured or shipped from a warehouse. The product is a set of ideas, images, and calculations rendered in a programming language.

When we combine these two dimensions, we find a whole world of different business types emerge. Here are nine examples, in their different positions:

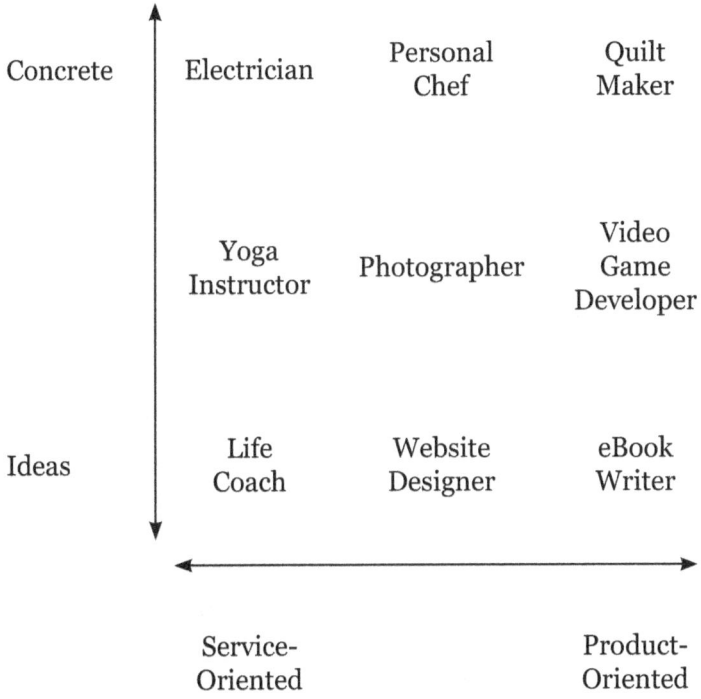

In the left column of this chart, we have service-oriented businesses. In the right column are product-oriented ones. At the top are businesses that are more focused on concrete, physical offerings. At the bottom are ideas-oriented businesses. In the middle sections we have various blends.

An important thing to note is that *only* the upper-right part of this chart involves expensive logistics like manufacturing, storage, transportation, and physical returns. These concrete product businesses often require the most financial investment.

I share this because when many people think about opening a business, they automatically jump to the upper-right section. They envision creating physical products, or opening a store to sell those types of products. As they begin to see price estimates for facilities and logistics, the business begins to feel daunting and they lose steam.

Because of that, I encourage my clients (especially those new to self-employment) to consider service-oriented businesses, or products that are less tangible. This can help ease the move into business ownership.

The lower-left section usually requires the least financial investment. People who provide *services* in the world of *ideas*—for example, academic tutors, marketing consultants, graphic designers, IT troubleshooters, executive coaches, sales leads generators, and so on—often require nothing but a phone and computer.

This can be an easy, affordable place to get started in the world of self-employment.

The Third Dimension

Finally, let me add a third dimension: the *number of people* involved in the business.

If you're planning to launch a sole proprietorship where you are the only employee, you're in good company. This is how most small businesses start.

However, some people don't want to go it alone; they begin by forming a partnership. In this case, you may have two or three people in your company.

Other people begin a business by immediately hiring contractors, consultants, or employees. In this case, you might have a team of people. Restaurants, for example, generally need a group of workers right up front.

If you'd like to dip your toe into the world of self-employment, you might want to focus on sole proprietorship businesses. Even if your business idea doesn't generate a great deal of money right away, you will be free of the pressure of paying employees.

Partnerships can be a fine way of starting as well, especially if one partner is the "financier" and the other partner(s) actively run the business. With partnerships, you'll feel less alone and will have help with growing the company.

And of course, there are many businesses that raise money and hire employees right off the bat. Generally this approach is taken by experienced entrepreneurs. However, your business might require a team in order to function.

Here is how the three dimensions form a "cube."

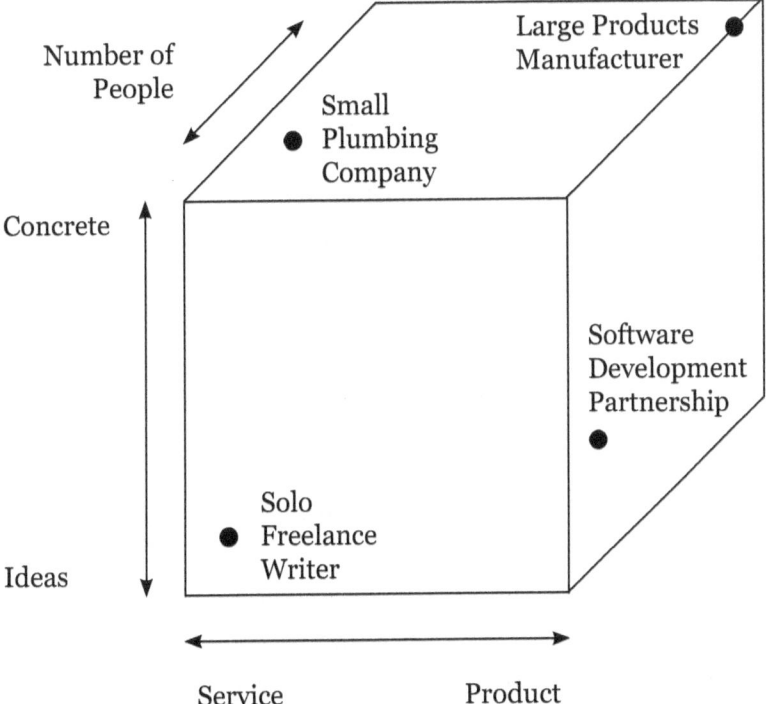

I've included four examples in different locations. There is a solo freelance writer, a pair of people developing software, a small plumbing company, and a large manufacturer of products.

As you can see, your business idea can fall anywhere within this cube: service or product, in the physical world or the world of ideas, with anywhere between one and many employees.

This three-dimensional approach is designed to help you expand your scope of consideration as you think about business ideas. If you have only been considering one corner or side of this cube, you might want to explore what a business in another section might look like.

Are you thinking about offering a service? If so, you might want to consider a product offering as well.

Are you considering a physical product? Perhaps there is a digital or ideas-oriented additional product that you can offer.

Are you planning to go it alone? If so, perhaps you can consider involving a consultant, a contractor, a partner, or eventually an employee.

Again, the best place to start is to identify needs that companies and people have. Then try to hold an open mind as you consider solutions for those needs.

Exploring various places in this cube—even just as an imagination exercise—can help to open up new business offerings. Especially at the beginning of running a business, it can be wise to have a diverse mix.

Marketing Your Business

Once you have chosen a product or service to offer, you will need to let your audience know what you are offering.

This is where newly self-employed people often get stuck.

I have had many conversations with my career counseling clients that went like this:

"So Sven," I say, "You've recently launched a massage therapy practice. How is it going?"

"Really slow," says Sven. "That's why I'm here to talk to you. I'm thinking about shutting it down."

"Not enough clients?"

"No, not at all. One a day maybe. Some days none at all."

"OK. Let's talk about what you've done to get your business visible. Do you have a website?"

"No. I'm not great with computers."

"Got it. Have you reached out to people who can give you referrals? Perhaps physical therapists?"

"That's a good idea, but I really don't know any PT's."

"Perhaps you can tell me what type of marketing and outreach work you've done."

"Well that's the thing—not much. I'm not good at marketing. I figured that I'd get word-of-mouth referrals from clients. That is happening, but it's very slow. Perhaps I'm just not cut out for running my own practice."

This situation is extremely common. I've had this type of conversation many times.

Especially for direct-service providers, there's often a tendency to believe that marketing will take care of itself. We have all heard, "If you build it, they will come"—but it's very difficult for an audience to find you if they don't know about your offering. That is where marketing and outreach comes in.

For clients of mine who dislike terms like "sales and marketing," I simply describe the outreach process as *communication*.

We are communicating about your products and services. We're not going to pressure or aggressively sales pitch anyone. We are simply going to let people know how your business can help with their needs.

Are there people around Sven who could use massage therapy? I'm sure there are! But they need to know what he is offering, and how it can help them in a beneficial way. Sven will need to devote some time to this type of communication.

Of course, he doesn't need to do this alone. Recall my cube from earlier: Sven is in the lower-left-front.

I would ask him to consider moving a bit deeper in the cube, perhaps by hiring a freelance website designer to develop a site for his practice. Or a graphic designer to create brochures. Or an internet ads consultant to help create some online ads. Or he can simply ask his friends to help him spread the word.

Sven doesn't need to do the marketing for his business alone. But he probably does need to devote some time (and possibly some money) to getting the communication flow going.

Specialization

As part of the communication process, a powerful step that can help your business stand out from the crowd is to create *specializations*.

Let's continue with our massage therapist. Sven, like many people in the healing arts, describes himself as "holistic." This means that he draws on many different traditions in his massage therapy work, and he's flexible in his approach.

While being holistic is great from a practice standpoint, it's not very helpful from a marketing perspective. If you describe yourself as "holistic," there's really no way to distinguish your offering.

One of the first things I'll discuss with Sven is creating a *specialty*.

For example, might he consider offering massage therapy services for corporations, on-site at the office? If so, that's a very unique specialty.

Or might he work with elder clients in their homes? Or with people returning from rock climbing injuries? Those are unique offerings.

Sven can have multiple specialties. Each one will help him communicate his business offerings in a way that is memorable, colorful, and specific. He can still remain open to all types of clients, but his specialties will help him develop his customer base.

As I've mentioned previously, the best way to start your business is to create custom-tailored solutions based on needs. Sven can talk to people and companies, and see if there are specific

SELF-EMPLOYMENT

needs he can fill. Then he can create specialties based on what he learns.

I encourage you to think about specialties. It will be far easier to get the word out about your business if you have a colorful set of unique offerings. Specialties will help people to remember you.

As a personal example, when I launched my counseling practice, I had a number of conversations like this:

"So you're a counselor?" someone would ask me.

"Yes, I specialize in both career counseling and cognitive behavioral therapy, which focuses on practical therapy tools," I would say. "I also work on a sliding-scale."

Now, that covered three different specialties:

1. Career counseling
2. Cognitive behavioral therapy, focusing on practical tools
3. Sliding-scale therapy

Almost every time I would say that, I'd get a strong reaction to one of those three:

"Career counseling? Hey, my son could really use help with his career. Can you help him with his resume?"

"Cognitive behavioral therapy? I read about that recently in a newspaper article. I actually have a friend who is looking for that type of therapy. Can I have your number?"

"That's great that you work on a sliding scale. My coworker could use help, but she doesn't have much money. Perhaps I can tell her about you."

By contrast, if I didn't have any specialties, the conversation might go like this:

"So you're a counselor?"

"Yes, I take a holistic approach."

"Holistic. Hmm. OK, sounds interesting. Good luck with your practice!"

Without the specialties, there's not much for the person to react to. She may not even know what "holistic" means. Even if she does, I'm just another person using that general term.

A large number of my self-employed clients fall into this trap. They don't have specialties, and so there is nothing for potential customers to grab on to.

Specialties will help you market your offering. Your specialties will stick in people's minds, especially if they are unique.

As I mentioned previously, it's best to start by talking to people and companies about their needs. Then you can consider which products or services you can offer to help with those needs. If you carve out specialties as you do this, your products and services will be much more memorable.

Marketing Action Steps

Getting to a point where "word of mouth" builds your business is a great goal. That was Sven's plan, and it's a wonderful place to aim for.

It's worth celebrating when your business grows to a point where people are singing its praises, and you don't have to work very hard (if at all) to get the message out about your offerings. However, to get to that point, you might need to invest some time, energy, and money to get the word out.

There are two primary ways of doing this, and I recommend using both:

1. Advertising (which I'm going to define very broadly)
2. Outreach to potential customers *and also to referral sources*

Let me start by discussing the value of advertising. Many of my entrepreneurial clients say, "Dan, I don't have money to run ads. I am barely covering my basic expenses."

SELF-EMPLOYMENT

I understand this. Advertising, as I'm using the term, doesn't need to involve expensive paid ads. There are countless other ways to communicate about your business offerings to a broad audience.

As an example, let me share what I did in the weeks before launching my counseling practice.

I created a counseling website with therapy information and self-help worksheets. I wrote an article about "mindfulness" practices and mentioned my counseling business at the end of the article. I created a blurb about my company for the place where I rented my office. I announced the opening of my practice in a newsletter of mine.

The total cost of all that was around $100. None of those were traditional ads. However, those advertising efforts immediately began to generate some client inquiries. In fact, I had two or three clients lined up before my office was even ready!

In the same way, you can think about ways to get the word out about your business offerings. You can write posts on social media sites. You can generate articles for websites related to your field. You can create a series of videos. You can make yourself available to be interviewed by journalists or podcasters. All this can be powerful (and free) advertising for your business.

For a small amount of money, you can also create a simple website. You can put together a tri-fold brochure and begin to hand that out to people. You can create a postcard and add it to a tackboard at a coffee shop. You can create a flyer and post it. There are countless ways to get the word out about your business.

"Dan, I might do all that work and only get a handful of clients," some people say to me. That's true. But those handful of clients can form a nucleus, and begin to generate the word-of-mouth buzz that you're seeking.

You can consider paid ads as well. Print ads in newspapers or magazines are usually quite expensive. Digital ads, by contrast, are often cheaper and allow you to target your message to particular audiences.

Digital ads often let you view exact metrics—the number of people who viewed your ad, the number who clicked on it, even demographics like age and location. This can help you to understand your audience and refine your message further. I know several businesses that were successfully built by using Google or Facebook ads.

You can also consider approaching a website owner to ask about "sponsoring" a site with an ad of yours. I have had people approach me to do this with several sites that I own. This can funnel visitors to your own site.

Outreach and Referrals

Let's now turn from advertising to an even more powerful form of marketing: direct outreach to customers and referral sources.

Let's say that I have a client named Elisabet who just opened a dog day care business. She has ten clients, but she would like to attract twenty or thirty more.

Advertising may be helpful. But Elisabet can also have direct conversations with dog owners—*and people who cross paths frequently with dog owners*. That second group of people can be a great source of referrals for her.

In our sessions, I would brainstorm with Elisabet about who these path-crossing people might be.

What type of person interacts with a large number of dog owners each day? These are people who might give Elisabet numerous customer leads.

Here's the type of list we might come up with:

1. Veterinarians and vet techs
2. Volunteers at animal shelters
3. Dog walkers

4. Pet sitters
5. People who run clubs for specific dog breeds
6. Employees at pet stores

There are plenty more options, but this list is a good start.

Elisabet can begin by developing a custom message to each of these types of people.

Vets and vet techs could be a great source of potential referrals. For them, Elisabet can clarify how safe and professional her daycare facility is, and explain how she cares for the dogs. She can describe how she and her staff members are trained to prevent injuries and resolve conflicts.

Volunteers at animal shelters are probably very sensitive to animal happiness. Elisabet can describe to them the enrichment and play activities that she provides at her daycare. She might invite these people to visit and observe how much fun the dogs are having.

Dog walkers are tricky, as these people might see a day care facility as a threat to their dog walking businesses. Perhaps Elisabet can form partnerships with these people, or offer to trade referrals. She might create an offering where walkers come by mid-day to take the dogs on neighborhood strolls.

And so on. Each of these people can become a referral source for Elisabet. If she is seeking to add twenty or thirty new clients, she might only need *two or three* enthusiastic referrers in order to hit those numbers.

Elisabet can also reach out directly to individual dog owners by meeting people at dog parks, volunteering at shelters, and chatting with neighbors and friends about her offerings. This one-on-one relationship building can be very impactful for small service-oriented businesses.

Product-oriented businesses can also reach out directly to potential customers. The best ones are very good at doing this.

For example, twenty years ago a friend of mine was hired to hand out free snack bars to people at a local fair. That snack bar company now sells around a billion dollars of products each year. Back when they were building their brand, they hired people to give out samples to individual people. They developed customers by handing out one free snack bar after another.

The long-term goal is to get to a point where your clients and customers sing your praises to others. But in order to get to that point, some outreach, marketing, and advertising efforts may be needed.

The Importance of Empathy

Let me conclude this chapter with a few therapy concepts that are related to self-employment.

One of the most important skills you can develop as an entrepreneur is what we therapists call "empathy."

In the world of psychology, empathy doesn't refer to compassion or sympathy. Empathy, as we use the term, is the *ability to see the world through other people's eyes*.

Almost every successful entrepreneur I've worked with has high empathy skills. They are able to view their business offerings through the eyes of their customers, suppliers, employees, and partners. They are able to adjust their messaging, products, services, and approaches for specific audiences.

When you're employed as a part of a company, you have a supervisor and a team of people who can give you feedback. But when you're self-employed, you may not have anyone to guide your decisions. Therefore, it's essential to learn how to perceive your business from the outside, as if you were a customer.

Empathy skills can make or break a business. I've worked with many highly intelligent, technically gifted people who were fairly tone deaf about how their communication style and activities impacted others. When some of these people started businesses, they made one "market reading" mistake after another. They were not skilled at viewing their business offerings from other peoples' perspectives.

The good news is that empathy skills, like any other skill, can be developed with practice. To help with this, I encourage you to relentlessly seek feedback from others as you start your business.

You can ask the people around you:

"What parts of this product appeal to you?"
"What changes might make it more appealing?"
"How does my website feel to you?"
"Does this product name grab you?"
"What do you think of the package design?"

Every time that you ask questions like those, you will be gathering real-world information of how your business looks to the public. Each new data point will help you to understand how people are responding to your business. You can then adjust things, and ask again.

The more you do this, the greater your capacity will be to see your company from an outside perspective. This will help you enormously in the process of marketing, developing new products and services, and responding to changing needs in the marketplace. These empathy skills can contribute to business success more than anything else.

Seeking the Win-Win

Finally, let me share what I consider to be the most important (and enjoyable) part of self-employment: the daily search for win-win solutions.

Self-employment can be like a giant game of hide and seek. You can spend your days seeking creative solutions that will benefit everyone that your business touches.

These mutually beneficial solutions are a "win" for you and a "win" for other people as well. It can be a great deal of fun to seek these win-win arrangements as you go through your day.

I spend a great deal of time with my entrepreneurial clients brainstorming win-win solutions. How can we bring happiness to employees, customers, clients, suppliers, landlords, and anyone else touched by the business? What creative arrangements will help everyone?

When you're working for an established corporation, there is usually a strict set of policies and procedures that you need to follow. But when you're running your own business, you're free to come up with endless unique solutions.

I find this to be the most enjoyable aspect of running a business: the freedom to bring happiness to people in limitless ways. I will cover this dynamic in the next chapter as well, as win-win solution finding can be a powerful method of improving your work life whether you're self-employed or not.

For now, let me answer some questions I've received about the path of self-employment.

CHAPTER ELEVEN

Self-Employment: A Deeper Look

In the last chapter, we covered the importance of identifying needs and creating products and services to meet those needs. We also explored various ways to market and advertise (or simply communicate about) your offerings.

Let me now share some questions that I've received about self-employment.

Q: I like the idea of being a "digital nomad" and traveling the world with my laptop, doing jobs over the internet. Do you have any thoughts about getting started with that type of business?

A: I know several people who successfully built a roaming freelance practice like you described. It's becoming a very viable form of self-employment.

All the principles that I described earlier are applicable to your situation. You will likely benefit by researching needs and desires of your potential client base, and then creating solutions to meet those needs. Outreach to potential clients and referral sources can be helpful. Even though you're probably considering service-oriented freelancing, you may be able to offer some products that can be delivered digitally as well.

Beyond those basics, I often recommend that my freelance clients become established on platforms like Upwork and Fiverr. These sites match freelancers with companies on a per-project basis. You will need to create a profile, and either "bid" on available projects, or wait for "buyers" to approach you. Feel free to experiment with different pitches, descriptions, and rates.

Once you have established yourself with a few happy clients, you can ask them for referrals. You can also ask if they would serve as references. In time, you might find that you have more work than you can handle.

If you're exploring what types of services to offer, I've included a list of some "careers that can be done remotely" in the last chapter of this book. However, as I mentioned, there is no substitute for having conversations with people about actual needs.

Feel free to ask any business owners you know what they could use help with. Then see if there's a way to help those people while living a digital nomad lifestyle.

Q: I'm a quiet person, and I just don't feel comfortable promoting my business. I'd rather people find their way to me. But I struggle to pay my bills, even though I do have a few happy customers and clients. Is there a way for us quiet people to run a business?

A: Quiet people can certainly run successful businesses. Let me return to the concept of "flipping the script" that I introduced earlier. You might find that this approach is more comfortable than conventional promotion.

As you may remember, when we flip the script, we shift from *getting* something (in this case, clients and customers) to *giving* enjoyably.

If you would like to develop a larger customer base, one approach is to increase your giving. Give out helpful information. Give away product samples. Give referrals. Help other business owners. Give and help, rather than push and promote, and see what occurs.

Let's return to Sven the massage therapist as an example. He has a lot of time on his hands. He enjoys giving massages. Here are some ways that he can increase his giving:

1. He can hand out coupons for free massages.
2. He can offer a free massage as an auction prize for non-profit fundraisers.
3. He can put together a website that shares information on various types of massage therapy modalities.
4. He can create videos demonstrating massage techniques.
5. He can offer to mentor new graduates of massage therapy programs.
6. He can give free massages to residents of assisted living homes.

And so on. There are limitless ways for Sven to give. As he fills his days giving, it is *extremely* likely that the ripple-effects of his generosity will help to grow his business.

He's not looking for quid pro quo arrangements, of course. He's giving freely, without expectation. But it's very likely that the people he gives to will "reflexively empathize" with his generous mindset. These people may very likely feel inspired to help him spread the word about his business.

I find that this giving approach works very well for people who are sensitive, quieter, or otherwise averse to "hype it up" approaches.

You will, of course, need to give in a way that feels comfortable to you. The goal is to find win-win arrangements, and not engage in self-sacrifice. But even a little giving goes a long way.

I encourage you to make a list like I did above, and begin to experiment with different types of giving. As you do that, you might find that your customer base naturally grows.

Q: I'm really not great with accounting and computers and other technical aspects of running a business. Is it even worth trying if you're not technical?

A: I know a large number of non-technical people who are successfully self-employed. Hardly any entrepreneurs I know are accounting gurus. Very few are skilled at IT issues or complex computer systems. So yes, there are certainly ways to run a business without being technically-inclined.

To begin, you will probably want to find an accountant to help you with both finances and various forms of paperwork—licenses and so forth. There are many solo practitioner accountants who are quite affordable.

You also might want to track down a computer person who can help you with websites, email, and other IT-related issues.

After that, you may be all set. Even though there are many technology-related entrepreneurs, the majority of entrepreneurs are not computer-oriented. Musicians, restaurateurs, writers, psychologists, gardeners, interior designers, store owners—few of these entrepreneurs are highly technical.

There is room for all types in the world of self-employment. If you explore some of the needs around you, you may find that many of those needs can be filled by someone who is skilled at creative and artistic solution-finding.

Q: I have a friend who made it big with his business. He always tells me that you have to give 100% if you go into business for yourself. But you're encouraging us to try out self-employment gradually. Who is right?

A: There are endless ways to engage in self-employment. It's up to you to decide what approach feels right for you.

I recommend enjoyable approaches to self-employment because as a therapist, my primary goal is to help people find happiness and a sense of peace. The path of self-employment can serve those goals. Other people have different priorities, and different levels of comfort with investment and risk.

If you do dip your toe in the self-employment waters gradually, you're in good company. It's very common for people to start a self-employment venture as a side job. In the old days, this was called "moonlighting"—working at a second job while the moon was up.

I know many consultants who have conventional full-time employment during the day, and then consult for other companies at night. I know freelancers who hold a part-time or full-time job in addition to their freelance work. Many people have "side gigs" that they run on the weekends. All these are perfectly valid ways to pursue self-employment.

As long as it doesn't threaten your current job (or violate a non-compete agreement), you too can begin to offer a product or service while continuing a normal job. If you start a side business, and it begins to take off, you'll need to decide how much of your time to devote to each of your activities.

Now, I do agree with your friend that larger businesses with multiple employees usually require a deep commitment of time, energy, and attention. You may indeed need to give 100% of your time if you're starting a business like a restaurant or a manufacturing company.

However, there is no rule that you need to aim for a large business. You can walk the self-employment path in whatever way appeals to you. There are countless "solopreneurs" with zero additional employees who have developed extremely robust businesses.

Q: I would actually love to have consultants and employees help me with my business. But I don't have much money to pay them. Do you have any suggestions?

A: There are many win-win arrangements that you can explore if money is tight.

For example, you can offer to pay sales people on contingency or commission. You can offer a partial ownership position in your business. You can offer your service as a "trade," in exchange for a reduced rate for someone else's service. (Though check with an accountant about tax implications on that.)

If you are ready to hire actual employees, you can consider part-time or as-needed work. You are not required to hire people on a full-time basis. If you're comfortable having people work at unusual hours, or on a per-project basis, you might be able to find plenty of people who would like to pick up some extra work.

If you're starting out on a minimal budget, you might want to hire consultants rather than employees—for example, marketing consultants or lead generators who can help you to increase your customer base. Feel free to check out Upwork and Fiverr, which I referenced earlier, to find an abundance of freelancers and consultants.

Seeking creative solutions is key. As I mentioned earlier, this creative problem-solving can be one of the most enjoyable parts of self-employment.

Q: Even though you recommend responding to needs, I'm not sure where to even begin asking people and companies about needs. Do you have some ideas for business ideas to get the ball rolling?

A: Sure. I've created a list of a few dozen business ideas in the last chapter of this book. Note that these types of lists are simply designed to open your mind to possibilities. I believe that your own inner compass will guide you toward options to explore.

Feel free to read through that list, and note if you feel a pull. Then begin to research whether there are needs for that type of business.

The actual conversations you have with people will the best source for business ideas.

·

Let me conclude the discussion of self-employment by summarizing the major themes that I covered.

Self-employment can be a wonderful journey of learning and growth. There is no real "failure" in self-employment; a business that doesn't make a lot of money can still be a stepping-stone to another part of your career path.

I recommend approaching self-employment with patience. Your first, second, or third business ideas might not "take." It's important to make peace with this in advance, and treat the process as a learning experience. I know several entrepreneurs who tried many business ideas before they found one that hit.

When you're considering business ideas, it's wise to start by assessing the needs of the people and companies around you. What are they needing help with? Where are they stuck? If you can create a business offering to help them, you will likely find a very ready customer base.

You can use the three-dimensional model to expand your vision of what to offer. If you have an idea for a service, is there a product that you can create as well? If you have a concrete offering, is there an ideas-based one you can add to the mix? Might it be helpful to involve consultants, contractors, partners, or employees to help you?

Once you have an offering, you can get the word out both through advertising and through direct outreach to customers and referral sources. Referrers can be extremely powerful. It may be helpful to come up with a list of potential referral sources, and create a custom message for each of them.

Specializations can be extremely valuable. If you specialize in certain areas or niches, it will help people to remember your offerings. It will also give referral sources a pitch to recommend you. You can have many specialties, and expand beyond them. But focusing at first on a handful of unique areas can give your business a boost.

Finding win-win solutions each day is an enjoyable part of self-employment. When you're running your own business, you can continually make "deals" that benefit both you and your customers, clients, employees, suppliers, and anyone else who is touched by your work. Seeking and finding these arrangements can be a fun game.

Let me now move on to the last chapter in this book: a discussion of how to improve your day-to-day work life, whether you're conventionally or self-employed.

CHAPTER TWELVE

Increasing Your Happiness at Work

When I opened my counseling practice, I expected to spend my time helping people find new careers.

To my surprise, it turned out that many of my clients decided to stay at their current jobs in the end. And why? Because as we explored their work lives, my clients discovered positive changes that could be made. They found ways to improve their job satisfaction.

In this chapter, I'll share five simple work-life improvement techniques that I use in my sessions. Even if you are seeking a new career, you can experiment with these five approaches in your present role. You may be able to increase your sense of fulfillment even while you explore new paths.

Before I begin, I want to acknowledge that the pace of work at many companies has become unsustainable. A large number of organizations have fallen into a pattern of laying-off employees and then increasing the workload of everyone who remains.

This has led to enormous stress, burnout, and a split in our economy. We have a group of people who are increasingly being worked to a breaking point. We have another group of people who are struggling to find sustainable employment.

Because of this trend, I want to state plainly that you will be walking a new path if you try the approaches in this chapter. You will be modifying an unsustainable pattern. You will be a trailblazer of sorts.

In this chapter, I will give a basic overview of five approaches I use with my clients. Then I will take a deeper look at these techniques through a series of questions.

First Approach:
Prioritize a Personal Goal

The first approach is simple.

Every morning, before you start your work for the day, you move a personal goal ahead of your professional goals.

Has your company hired you to make a sale, complete a task, or manage a team? If so, those are secondary goals. We're going to jump the line and move a primary goal ahead of that.

Your top goal is to *do your work in a way that is enjoyable to you*. That goal jumps ahead of all others. Everything else comes after.

Some people stop me at this point and say, "Dan, I'll get fired if I try to do my work in an enjoyable way. My company doesn't care about my happiness at all."

I certainly respect your choices, and don't want you to risk losing your job. However, many companies are quickly learning that unhappy employees are eventually going to jump ship for more fulfilling jobs.

When employees leave, companies have to hire recruiters to find new people—often at higher salaries than before. It is an enormous expense in time and money.

By setting the goal of working in an enjoyable way, you are actually *helping* your company. You are increasing your clarity of mind, reducing your chance of burnout, and maximizing the positive emotional impact that you'll have on your coworkers and customers.

Perhaps you are already working for an employer that values employee happiness. If so, that's wonderful. However, even in that case, it can still take some effort to prioritize work enjoyment.

Let me share how this dynamic plays out in my life.

Often when I wake up in the morning, my first thought is, "I have to respond to all these emails!"

Or, "I have to get going on those projects!"

Or, "I have to return my phone calls from yesterday!"

Those goals rush in immediately, often when I'm still half asleep.

At that point I pause and say, "No. Those are not my primary goals for today. My primary goal is to do my work in a way that is enjoyable and emotionally healthy."

Throughout the day, my goals jockey back and forth for priority in my mind. Work in a way that's enjoyable? Or get as many projects done as quickly as possible? Which is most important?

I have to continually keep things aligned in the proper order. The top goal is to do my work in an enjoyable and healthy way. The secondary goal is anything else.

This draws on a fundamental principle in cognitive behavioral therapy. Our thoughts about our work—including the *dominant goals* we hold throughout the day—shape our emotional experience.

The mind will follow whatever goal we choose. If we want to find happiness in our work, we need to begin by setting that as a top priority. The mind is a faithful follower. It will travel along the path we set for it.

Now, to be clear: A goal is an aim. It is not a rigid rule. Your aim—your intention—is to approach your work in a way that is enjoyable and emotionally healthy. There's no pressure for you to "hit" that goal, and you may have many days when your work is anything but enjoyable.

Top Goal
To work in a way that is enjoyable and healthy
Secondary Goals
Everything else, including any professional goals

That is OK. You're simply setting the goal of finding happiness in your work, and making that a priority. The mind will follow your decision as you practice holding that direction.

Some of my clients say, "Dan, this all sounds unethical. My company is paying for my time. I have to do what they want me to do, even if it makes me miserable."

I say to them, "If you sacrifice your happiness for your company, you're going to eventually burn out, and then you won't be able to help your company or anyone else. In the long run, it helps your company if you work in a way that's enjoyable to you. It doesn't help them if you exhaust yourself, get fed up, and quit."

Let me give a real life example about this dynamic, so you don't think that I'm simply tossing out self-help platitudes. I recently conducted several recruiting searches for a company that lost numerous employees due to exhaustion, overwork, and unhappiness.

In addition to my recruiting costs, the company ended up having to pay thousands of dollars in higher salaries for the new employees. While I was recruiting new people, other employees at the company had to shoulder the departed folks' work, which created even more stress.

Over the coming months, the new people will have to be trained. Work will slow. Plus the former employees were very well-liked. They are already missed by their coworkers, some of whom are considering resigning themselves.

This is an *incredible* loss to the company in money, morale, and momentum. That company is now establishing a retention committee and working with a consultant to improve employee happiness at work. They learned the cost of not valuing their employees' fulfillment as a top goal.

You deserve to be happy in your work. Your company will benefit if you are happy. Burnout and misery doesn't help you or your company.

INCREASING YOUR HAPPINESS

Reminders

To support this new prioritization of goals, I often share "reminders" with my counseling clients. These reminders are thoughts that you can repeat throughout the day to help keep the mind on track.

Here are a few reminders that can help with the prioritization of work fulfillment:

> "I'll be able to come up with creative solutions more easily if I'm enjoying my work."
> "If I'm burned out, I won't be able to help anyone."
> "I'll be more helpful to my customers if I'm enjoying what I do."
> "It's OK to not give 100% every single minute of the day."

And so on. In my sessions, we come up with dozens of messages like these. All of them are designed for one simple purpose: to place the goal of happiness at the top.

"But Dan," some people say, "you don't know my boss. He doesn't care if I'm happy. All he cares about is getting the work done. He's perfectly fine if I'm miserable."

There are thousands of bosses like that out there. Perhaps millions. That is why I opened this chapter by acknowledging that we're blazing a new path with this approach.

If your company doesn't care about your long-term health, and simply wants to squeeze as much work out of you before you collapse in exhaustion—well, you'll have to decide whether that's a company you want to work for.

I have seen enough people collapse. I myself have collapsed enough times. There is no benefit to have workers collapsing. That is when mistakes are made that risk lives and money. I have seen errors made by exhausted workers that cost companies fortunes.

A work culture of burnout and misery doesn't serve anyone. Company success is built on employee health and happiness. A company and its people rise and fall together.

Training the Mind

Now, I'm sure that you've heard ideas like these before. Here's what makes the approach I'm describing different: I'm not recommending that you simply read through these ideas. I'm recommending that you *train your mind through repeated practice* to hold this new direction.

That is the essence of cognitive therapy. We're not going to engage in a few stray moments of positive thinking. Instead, we're going to form a disciplined practice of reorienting the mind over and over throughout the day, until a new habit is formed.

I encourage you to set aside a minute before you start your work day and say to yourself, "Today, my top goal is to do my work in a way that's enjoyable. Every other goal comes after that." Try to focus on that commitment for a minute or so.

Then, as you go through your day, notice when you lose a sense of peace. That might happen in the first five minutes of your workday!

When that happens, stop for a few seconds and say, "My primary goal is to do this work in an enjoyable, healthy way."

The first day, you might have to stop twenty or thirty times to remind yourself of your new priority. It might feel like a chore. You might not feel any big boost in happiness. But you're carving out a new path to follow with your practice.

The next day, you might find that it's a little easier to remember—and adhere to—your new goal.

After a week, you might find that a habitual response kicks in. A client is upset about something, and your mind remembers, "My top goal isn't to soothe this client. I will do that as best as I can, but my *top* goal is to do my work in an enjoyable way."

Paradoxically, that will very likely allow you to address your client's needs more effectively. It will calm your mind and allow you to access creative solutions more easily. By valuing your own happiness, you will be able to bring happiness to others—including your customers, your coworkers, and even your boss.

"Dan, this all sounds fine in theory," some people say to me. "But I have no idea *how* to do my work in a way that's enjoyable. It's not enough to just set a goal."

I agree.

Let me turn to the next approach, which ties in with the first.

Second Approach:
Seek Mutually Beneficial Solutions

Setting the top goal of work enjoyment isn't meant to create a conflict between you and your company. Quite the opposite. It places things in a correct order, so both you and your company can benefit.

Once the new priority is set, you can then focus on applying your goal. How can you do your work in an enjoyable way? What is the strategy to accomplish that?

My answer to that is the second of my five approaches. It is a technique I covered earlier. The second practice is this:

You can spend your days seeking, asking for, and proposing solutions that benefit *both you and your company.*

I call these "win-win solutions." However, if the term win-win sounds like corporate jargon, you can simply call them "mutually beneficial arrangements" or "solutions that work for everyone" or something similar.

As an example, here is a scenario that many of my clients have faced at times.

Imagine that your supervisor asks you to take on a new responsibility. You're already extremely busy, and this added work feels as though it will put you over an edge.

Your manager says to you, "I need you to set aside whatever you're doing and get right on this!"

You know that if you do that, your other responsibilities will stack up. You might even get blamed for falling behind on your other work.

Many people do one of two things at this point:

1. They grit their teeth in frustration and add the new responsibility to their ever-growing work pile.
2. Or they argue with their supervisor about why this is an unfair request.

Neither of those approaches are very enjoyable. The first option usually leads to exhaustion and resentment. The second option typically leads to debates and conflicts.

A third alternative is to ask for—and propose—solutions that work for both you and your company.

As an example, you might say to your supervisor:

"I'd be happy to handle this new project. However, can you help me figure out who may be able to help with the other projects on my plate? If no one can help, perhaps we can bump a few of them to next week. Can you help me find a solution?"

You're asking for help to find a win-win arrangement. You'll do the immediate project, but you'll need help to address your other responsibilities.

Let's imagine that your supervisor isn't having any of that. She says, "No! We don't have anyone else who can help you! And this all needs to get done! You'll have to find a way to do it all."

That's not a win-win solution. It might be a "win" for the company, but it's not a "win" for you.

So you make one more attempt at a mutually beneficial solution:

"I'd love to be able to take care of everything," you say, "but there simply aren't enough hours in the day. Let me suggest a

INCREASING YOUR HAPPINESS

couple of options. We can ask Bethany to help out with the paperwork which will free up some time. Or we can tell that new customer that we need to delay the shipment by a day. Or we can see if Merrill can come in to help us this afternoon, even though she's not scheduled. You might have some even better ideas. I'm open to your thoughts."

By taking this approach, you are proposing creative, specific, win-win solutions. In my experience, the majority of managers (not all, but the majority) appreciate this type of problem solving attempt.

Of course, there are some managers that will say, "I told you no! You can look for another job if you can't handle everything yourself!"

When clients report to me that their managers are in that mindset, I generally try to help them find a new job. (Usually I hear later that the insensitive manager was fired because she was making everyone miserable.)

However, quite frequently, many managers will say something like, "Those are good ideas. Let's choose the first option."

Or, "I'm not sure those will work, but how about we try this other option that's similar..."

By suggesting win-win solutions, you are helping yourself and the company. You're also showing your manager an excellent management technique.

Now, let me admit that this is not always easy. There is no quick script for cooperative problem-solving. Finding these arrangements can take effort and creativity.

I have spent countless hours with my counseling clients in attempts to find win-win solutions. I have helped them analyze their work situations in detail, make lists of specific proposals, and role-play the communication of those proposals.

Many of these clients were employees who felt micromanaged and controlled by their supervisors. But others were executives and managers who genuinely wanted to bring happiness to their employees. These executives were exhausted and overwhelmed themselves, and they needed help to find win-win arrangements.

If you can propose mutually beneficial solutions, it's a gift. Hopefully your supervisor will appreciate your efforts, and join you in cooperative problem-solving. If not, she will likely lose some very good employees.

The Combination

Combining the first and second techniques, here is how your work day looks:

For a minute at the start of your day, you say to yourself, "My top goal is to do my work in a way that is enjoyable."

During the day, when you feel your stress levels increasing, you take a moment to remind yourself that your goal is to work in an enjoyable, emotionally healthy way. Then you examine the project or task in front of you, and consider mutually beneficial ways of accomplishing the work.

You propose win-win solutions to your manager, client, or customer. You also invite win-win proposals from them. There may be some creative brainstorming that's required in this process. However, you might be surprised at how quickly solutions emerge once two people are cooperatively aiming for them.

As you seek solutions, you can make statements like:

"I'd love to find a solution here that makes everyone happy."
"I'm confident that we can find a way to do this that everyone feels good about."
"Let's see if we can put our heads together and figure out an arrangement that works."
"I love finding solutions. Here are a few options to consider."
"I want to make sure that we do this in a way that benefits everyone."

INCREASING YOUR HAPPINESS

I use statements like these quite often throughout my own day.

When I have a hiring manager with unrealistic expectations, or a therapy client who is resistant to change, I lean on these type of statements over and over. In the majority of cases, the other person appreciates my attempts to find solutions, and eventually joins me in the process.

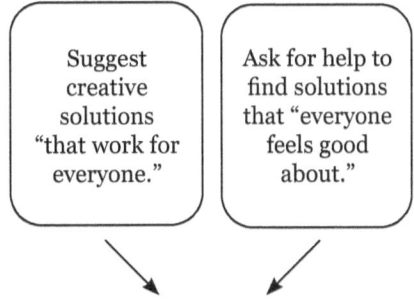

Cooperative, win-win problem solving

Again, I do want to acknowledge that there are managers out there who will say, "Stop complaining! Do what I tell you to do!"

I have known plenty of people like that. Those people usually end up alienating their employees, their customers, and sometimes even their friends and family.

If you are working for someone like that, you may want to draw on all the other chapters of this book to find a new employment situation with wiser leaders who value your happiness.

Increasing Challenges

So far, I've been focusing primarily on reducing burnout and exhaustion. However, what if you're not overwhelmed, but *bored?* This same win-win seeking approach can be used if you're under-stimulated as well.

If you're feeling unchallenged or under-utilized at work, you can propose new projects, responsibilities, and initiatives that are win-win arrangements. Choose things that are interesting to you. Then help your employer see how the company will benefit by you taking on these new initiatives.

Almost every "rising star" employee I've met is very skilled at this type of win-win proposal practice. These people frequently suggest new, interesting projects for themselves—often as a "trade" for less-interesting work. They show the company how it will benefit from the new projects.

They tackle their new responsibilities in an enjoyable way, show the company the beneficial results, and are often compensated more highly for their contributions. It can be a powerful way to advance a career. I encourage you to think about "trades" like this, where you propose interesting new projects in exchange for less-impactful work.

Now, what if your boss and your specific work responsibilities aren't the problem? What if you experience stress no matter where you are working, or what you are doing?

In that case, let me share a third approach to increase your happiness at work.

Third Approach:
Alter Your Locus of Control

As you may recall from a previous chapter, "locus of control" is a psychological concept that involves your view of the world.

People with a very *large* locus of control see themselves as being in control of almost everything in their lives.

While this fosters a sense of empowerment, it also creates an enormous amount of pressure. After all, if you're in control of thousands of things—well, you better get to work taking care of all of them!

By contrast, people with a very *small* locus of control see themselves as being in control of very little in their lives.

This worldview leads to feelings of powerlessness. However, it also reduces a sense of pressure. If you are not in control of very much, then there's really no urgency to expend effort. You can just float along and roll with whatever shows up.

The majority of clients I've worked with have a large locus of control. These people feel responsible for excelling at their

INCREASING YOUR HAPPINESS

work, building their businesses, retaining their employees, keeping their families happy, contributing to their communities, and many other things.

While those goals are admirable, an overly-large locus of control can create debilitating stress, anxiety, pressure, and exhaustion.

In the workplace, many companies encourage an extremely large locus of control.

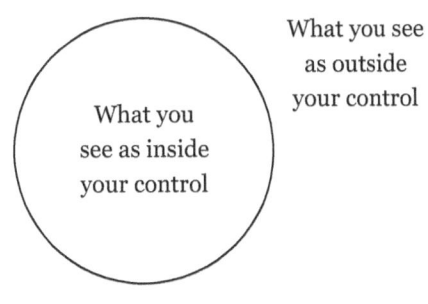

A manager might say to you, "I have faith that you can get all of these projects done on-time and under-budget!"

Or, "I'm sure that you can double our sales this year!"

On the surface, those sound like great votes of confidence. Most people don't question those type of statements. They simply internalize the "positive" messages, and expand their locus of control.

"Thanks, you bet I can!" they say.

However, you might be in a situation where it's impossible to get your ever-growing list of responsibilities done on-time and under-budget. It might be impossible to double sales in the current economy. There might be factors beyond your control that are in play.

In that case, you will probably become consumed with a sense of pressure and overwhelm as you try desperately to control things that are beyond your scope.

I have seen many examples of this in counseling. Employees are told that they can control things. They struggle to achieve things that are un-achievable. They become overwhelmed with a sense of exhaustion and failure as they are unable to meet expectations. Finally they give up and quit. This doesn't help anyone.

Just a Thought

The good news is that the locus of control is simply a set of beliefs. As such, it can be changed with a thought. Even though the mind often clings to its beliefs, you can make healthy changes in gradual steps.

I have had conversations with many high-achieving clients that went like this:

"Dan," says my client, "I'm ready to quit my job. I'm just completely burned out. I can't take it much longer."

"Tell me what's going on."

"Well, I'm trying to get all my projects done, but I can't hit my deadlines. I don't know what my problem is."

"What if it's *impossible* to get all your projects done in the time you've been given?" I ask.

"Impossible? I refuse to think that way. That sounds like a cop-out."

"Surely there's a limit to what you can get done in a day."

"If these are my projects, then they're my responsibilities. I have to get them all done."

"But what will happen if your company keeps adding even more projects to your plate?"

"Well, I guess I'll have to figure out how to handle them all somehow."

And the conversation goes from there. You can see that my client firmly believes that she can—and should—get all of her projects done, no matter how large a stack the company places on her desk.

But what if she's at, or beyond, her limit? What if the deadlines are too tight? What if she needs help or resources? What if there simply aren't enough hours in the day to get these projects done?

It can be far more healthy for my client to adjust her locus of control downward.

I will try to help her see that perhaps she can't make *everything* happen by the deadline—and that she's still a wonderful person and a wonderful teammate, regardless of that.

I will try to help her accept that there are some things beyond her ability to control, and that she doesn't need to pressure or criticize herself because of that. As she reduces her locus of control in a healthy way, she will very likely begin to feel a greater sense of peace.

Will this feel like a "cop-out" to her? Perhaps at first.

But recall our first two techniques:

We want to do our work in an enjoyable way. Unrelenting self-pressure isn't enjoyable.

We also want to find win-win solutions that benefit both us and our companies. Struggling and failing to meet unrealistic expectations doesn't benefit either party.

I encourage you to reset your locus of control in a way that is empowering on the one hand, and de-pressuring on the other.

As an example of this, here's the spiel I often give to corporate clients of mine when I begin working with them as a recruiter.

I say, "I am tenacious in my recruiting work. But recruiting often comes down to timing. If I call someone who just had a fight with her boss, she'll probably be delighted to hear about new jobs. If she just got a promotion, she probably won't talk to me at all. That's beyond my control. All I can do is continue my outreach patiently and persistently."

Most of my clients are fine with this. They see the wisdom in an accurate locus of control.

In the same way, I encourage you to examine the areas of your work life that are causing you overwhelm.

Do you believe that you have to control things that are not fully in your control—for example, other people's thoughts and feelings? Or the state of the economy? Or what your competition is doing? If so, you might want to examine and change those beliefs.

Most of my high-achieving clients are extremely resistant at first when I present these ideas. They say, "But I *can* change people's thoughts and feelings! And I'm *not* going to be stopped by the economy or my competition!"

While there's an admirable element of empowerment there, there's also a recipe for burnout. Some things are largely within our control, and others are not. Being humble about this can be the key to reducing pressure and exhaustion at work.

The Shovel and the Rock

Let me share how the locus of control concept applies to one of the most challenging dynamics in the work world.

Some companies set very high expectations for their employees. At the same time, the companies don't give their employees adequate *resources* to meet those expectations.

Instead, they simply try to increase their employees' loci of control through "pep talks." This creates an unhealthy dynamic.

Imagine, for example, that you've been asked to dig a ten foot hole. But you haven't been given any tools. You've simply been told, "You can do it! You can dig this hole! I have confidence in you. You can get it done!"

In that scenario, employees feel defeated and guilty when they can't dig the hole quickly, and end up hating their jobs. All the while, managers keep saying, "You can do it! Yes you can!"

In these situations, it can be helpful to accurately adjust your locus of control, and communicate that to your supervisor.

You can say, "Without a shovel, I might be able to use that rock over there to dig the hole. But it will probably take a week. If I have a shovel, I can probably do it in a day. Can we purchase a shovel so that I can do the work more quickly?"

In my experience, the majority of managers will appreciate an honest statement of your locus of control, especially if there are win-win solutions proposed.

One of the greatest mistakes I have made in my own work life has been to say, "Thanks for the confidence in me! I'll go ahead and get that hole dug with that rock! You bet I can do it!"

I wish I had instead said, "I really need a shovel."

If it feels as though you're being asked to control outcomes, but are not being given the tools to do so, please consider proposing solutions. Do not simply buy in to the expansion of your locus of control.

You deserve the resources you need to accomplish your tasks. It is not in your best interest—*or* your company's best interest—to have you feel defeated and disappointed when results aren't achieved.

Expanding a Small Circle

For some people, the locus of control is skewed in the opposite direction.

I've had clients who had very small loci of control. They felt that very little was within their power to change. This led to feelings of hopelessness and defeat.

When I work with clients like these, I help them to expand their locus of control—expand what they perceive as alterable.

We begin by looking for thoughts that say, "It's pointless to try to change this. Nothing will work. Why even bother."

We then substitute new thoughts like, "Perhaps I can try to make a *small shift* in just this *one* area." As a support for that new thought, we add in some small-step behaviors to try. Very frequently, these clients find that they can indeed effect changes and improvements.

If you feel disempowered in your work life, you may want to expand your locus of control. You can try on thoughts that say, "Perhaps I can make a slight change in this one situation," and then begin to experiment with small behavioral experiments.

It's very likely that—with help—you can change far more in your work life than you realize, even if changes happen one small step at a time.

Let me now move on to a technique for people who work in high-activity, fast-paced jobs. I use this fourth approach with my health care clients, as well as people who work in retail, customer service, operations, or other relentlessly busy environments.

Fourth Approach:
Break Ups

Many of my clients experience chronic, extremely high levels of job-related stress. These people deal with insomnia, dreams about work, feelings of guilt about not accomplishing more, and damaging impacts on their personal and professional relationships.

When these people describe their work lives to me, it's clear that no amount of "positive thinking" is going to improve their situation. The pace of their work environments is truly overwhelming. They need concrete behavioral changes.

I usually begin my work with these people by drawing the following diagram:

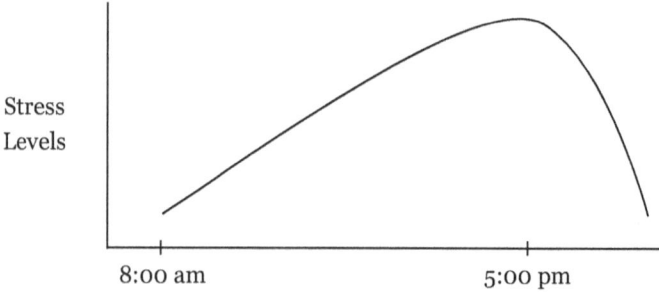

I ask them if this looks like an accurate depiction of their stress levels throughout the day.

Most of them say, "Oh yeah. I'm usually OK first thing in the morning. But then one thing after another piles up, and by the end of the day I'm shaking with stress and exhaustion. I can't keep this up."

I say to them, "I'd like to have you try a simple practice. I call it breaking up with your work. Starting tomorrow, I'd like you to take a break *every hour* for at least a few seconds. At those times, I want you to put your work aside, and allow your mind to get a moment of rest. It's essential to let those stress circuits release for at least a few seconds every hour."

I then draw a diagram like this:

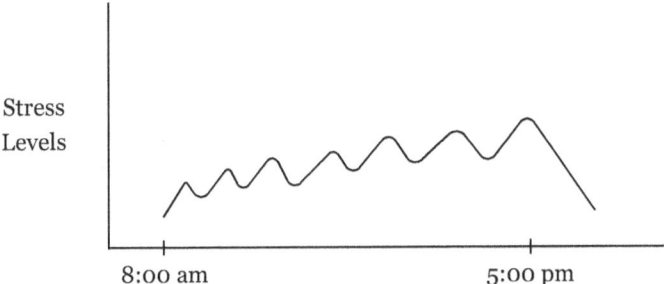

I say, "If you pause every hour to let your stress circuits release, you may find that your overall sense of exhaustion and overwhelm is less at the end of the day. Perhaps we can try that as an experiment, and see how things go."

You can see that this person's stress levels are still higher at 5:00 pm than they were at 8:00 am. However, the trajectory of increase is softer. By taking "break up" points every hour, this person has let her mind calm at regular intervals. For people in high-stress jobs, this can make a significant impact.

Like any other approach I've discussed, this needs to become an actual, practiced habit. It's not enough to say, "Sure, I should take a few breaks." It's essential to engage in the practice in a disciplined, repeated way.

We're retraining the mind to follow a new direction with this practice. We're forming a new pattern. Eventually that pattern can become a habit that mostly runs on its own. Getting to that point, however, requires committed behavioral practice.

To assist with the development of this habit, I often recommend that my clients purchase a lap counter for runners, and make a "click" each time they practice. I encourage them to write down the number of times they take breaks each day, and then bring their practice record to sessions for us to discuss. That can help in the formation of the habit.

Let me share a caveat about this practice: Even though it sounds simple, the mind is often *extremely resistant* to this type of practice.

One reason for the resistance is that our stress circuitry is essentially the same as our threat circuitry. When the mind is in a state of stress, it feels threatened by almost everything—including the act of stopping and quieting down. The stressed mind is actually frightened of rest.

Each time you engage in a break-up practice, you are saying to your mind, "I'm not going to feed this sense of threat, pressure, and stress. I am going to take a few moments and give myself a rest—even if it feels difficult."

I encourage you to actually try this tomorrow, and see how many breaks you get. If you are able to stop every hour for a brief rest, you are among a very small group of people!

If instead you find that you only remember to pause and rest a few times during the day—well, that's still a great start. Build on that with another day of practice, and another.

See if you can work up to eight or ten breaks throughout your work day, each lasting up to a minute or so.

What to Do?

Let's say that you are indeed able to pause and take a break to let your stress circuits relax. What should you do during these rest times?

One practice you can try is what I call the "waves technique." This is a mindfulness-style practice. In the waves technique, you stop, close your eyes if possible, and pretend that you're standing waist-deep in the ocean.

Your stressful feelings are like waves that are knocking up against you. For a few seconds, allow those feelings to flow up to you and past you as you hold your center. Try to feel the sense of calm that lies *between* the waves as you give permission for each of the feelings to pass through you.

In addition to feelings, you might find that there are stressful thoughts that knock against you as well. Thoughts like:

"I have to get this project done!"
"I really don't have time to stop."
"What if someone sees me not working?"
"This is a dumb practice! I hate it!"

Allow those thoughts to pass through your awareness, just like your feelings. Allow your mind to rest in a quiet center, even for just a second or two at a time, as you allow the stressful feelings and thoughts to rise up in your awareness, and then pass by.

This type of practice can be difficult at first. It might feel as though you're being barraged by an endless number of waves without a break in between. But as you practice letting those waves rise up in your awareness and then pass through, you will likely find a space emerge between each one.

That space is our goal. That space is the point at which the stress circuits relax and release. Even just a few seconds spent in that space can have a stress-lowering effect.

Let me state once again that this isn't simply a self-help technique; it is a disciplined practice. It is a mind-training process. It is a new habit.

You may need to engage in hundreds of these break-up moments before you begin to feel a change in your day-to-day stress levels. The effort and persistence is worth it.

If the waves technique doesn't appeal to you, you can use whatever approach brings you a sense of peace during your break times. The act of stopping is the important thing. You can use whatever restorative practice appeals to you during that time.

I know of people who take walks around the building, or up a flight of stairs. Some people open an inspirational book and read a paragraph or two. Others look at a calming photo of nature or their family.

I encourage you to experiment and see what you find.

Fifth Approach:
Choosing a Purpose

The final practice is one that I introduced at the very beginning of this book: choosing a purpose for your work.

In my experience, very few people consider *why* they are doing the specific type of work that they do. Establishing a purpose can have a powerful emotional effect.

I often have conversations like this with my counseling clients:

"So Thom," I say, "it sounds as though you're not happy with your current career path. I'm curious if you've ever chosen a purpose—or mission—for your work life. Is that something you've thought about?"

"Not sure what you mean," says Thom.

"In addition to earning money, is there a personal reason that you do the type of work you do?"

"No real reason. It's just a job."

"If we can select a meaningful purpose that your work serves," I say, "your entire experience of your career might shift. Is that something that we can discuss?"

"Sure Dan, but I basically do what my boss tells me. There's no higher purpose."

This is where my conversations jump to a deeper place. Thom doesn't have to defer to his boss's purpose for his work. He can choose his own purpose or mission that brings him a sense of fulfillment.

I will ask Thom about his values. I'll ask about his world views. I'll try to learn about his personal philosophy of life. Hopefully, we'll be able to come up with a purpose for his work (in addition to making money) that places his activities in a new, meaningful context.

Here are a few purpose statements that I might explore with Thom:

"The purpose of my work is to bring happiness to the people around me."
"The purpose of my work is to practice being kind."
"The purpose of my work is to keep people safe."
"The purpose of my work is to develop my skills."
"The purpose of my work is to support my family."

That last one is a very common purpose, and it is a great one. You may already have a purpose like one of those.

However, based on my experience, many people don't have a purpose established for their work beyond, "Just pay the bills."

Earning money is a perfectly valid purpose. But you can earn money at any number of jobs. To bring a sense of meaning to your work, you might want to fill that purpose slot with a specific mission that supports your values.

Recall my stories at the beginning of this book. I felt extremely unfulfilled by my early jobs at the computer store, the road paving company, the urban planning organization, and the manufacturing firm.

Part of that was because they were unstimulating jobs in isolating environments. But I also had a complete lack of purpose beyond simply getting through the day.

These days, I understand how crucial it is to hold a well-defined purpose. I try to keep statements of purpose front and center in my mind. For example:

> **My Work Purpose:**
>
> You get to fill this with whatever you choose.
>
> As you fill this purpose slot, you will be setting a direction for your work life.
>
> Your emotional experience of work will tend to follow this.

My purpose in my counseling work is to help people find a sense of happiness as quickly as possible, and to give them tools so that they can "be their own therapists."

My purpose in my recruiting work is to help build teams of people in a way that benefits both employees and employers.

My purpose in my writing is to share helpful information as widely and clearly as possible.

I enjoy all three facets of my work life because of the purposes I have set.

Of course, it's not enough to simply choose a purpose; we need to frequently remind ourselves of the purpose we've set, and realign our work with that purpose if it has drifted away. Keeping on track is an ongoing process.

Our emotional experience of our work will follow the direction we set for it. I encourage you to set a purpose or mission for your work that brings you a sense of fulfillment. The choice of purpose is up to you.

Recap

Before I move on to the Q&As for this topic, let me recap how you can use the five techniques we covered.

At the beginning of your work day, you can take a few moments to move a personal goal ahead of any professional goals. Your personal goal is to do your work in a way that is enjoyable to you. When you feel yourself becoming unhappy during the day, you can remind yourself what your top goal is, and reset the priorities.

To serve this goal, you can become a win-win solution seeker. You can propose mutually beneficial solutions that help you *and* your company. You can also ask for these solutions from others. You may want to use phrases like, "I'd like to find a solution that works for everyone."

If you feel overwhelmed and pressured by demands, you can adjust your locus of control downward and remind yourself that there are elements of life that are largely beyond your control—including things like the economy, your competitors' actions, and the number of hours in a day.

In areas where you feel powerless to make changes, you can expand your locus of control outward by reminding yourself that you *can* influence a number of things, at least in small ways. You can then try various experiments to make these incremental changes.

Throughout the day, you can pause and allow your stress circuits to relax. For best results, you can do this every hour.

During these "break up" times, which may only be a few seconds, you can use the waves technique to allow your feelings and thoughts to pass through your awareness. Or you can engage in any other stress-reduction technique that appeals to you. Simply forming the habit of taking regular breaks is the key.

Above all else, you can set a higher purpose or mission for your work.

You can ask yourself: What is the reason that I am doing this work? What purpose do I want it to serve? You are in control of that decision.

If you choose a purpose that supports your values, you may find that your work life takes on a new emotional tone. You may begin to feel a deeper sense of fulfillment as all your activities fall into alignment with your stated mission.

Let me now move on to some Q&As on this topic.

CHAPTER THIRTEEN

Increasing Your Happiness at Work: A Deeper Look

The five approaches from the last chapter can be a good foundation to make changes at work. However, there are limitless ways to apply these approaches, and you may need to be very creative in your application.

To expand the presentation of these five techniques, let me share some of the questions I've received about them.

Q: I'm not sure what you mean by doing your work in a way that's enjoyable. What does that look like exactly?

A: The answer to this question will be unique to you. You get to decide what an enjoyable experience of work looks like.

Some people need different pacing in their work—slower pacing for some, but faster and more challenging pacing for others. Some people want to take on fewer projects, or more. There are folks who need tools to help them do their work more effectively. Others want to increase their learning, development, and growth.

Many people these days are finding that remote or hybrid work arrangements help them to feel happier in their work. Or more flexible hours. Or more feedback from their managers. Some people want increased social contact and bonding at work; others want more alone time in order to focus.

There is no single answer to this question. In fact, you might find that you'll need to make a variety of small shifts throughout the day in order to increase your happiness at work. That is why setting an overall goal, and maintaining that goal as a priority, is more important than making one or two modifications.

My recommendation is to begin by asking yourself what changes might help to increase your work enjoyment *just for today*.

Then try to envision how you could make those changes (or frame requests for those changes) in a way that will benefit your company as well as yourself. Continue that as a day-to-day practice until it becomes a habit.

Q: When you talk about setting work enjoyment as your top priority, it sounds as though you're telling people to slack off. How is that a good thing?

A: Funny enough, some of my best therapy sessions involved telling overworked people that it's OK to slack off a bit!

But slacking off isn't the goal. The goal of this approach is to restore peace to your mind so that you can be a fulfilled, high-contribution team member—*and* a happy person. That's a success for both you and your company.

I have known people (including some high-level executives) who did the opposite of what I'm recommending. These people prioritized their work goals over their own happiness. In their drive to accomplish those goals, they became exhausted, angry employees who ended up alienating their coworkers.

When these people were let go from their jobs, they were shocked. After all, they had sacrificed everything for their work.

What they didn't realize is that by mis-prioritizing their own happiness, they ended up upsetting everyone around them—and contributing to an unpleasant, high-stress work culture. If they had maintained a daily goal of doing their work in a way that was peaceful and enjoyable, they would have helped both the company and themselves.

Recall that the goal of work enjoyment is coupled with win-win solution finding. If you make it a priority to do your work in an enjoyable way, and then propose win-win arrangements to serve that goal, you'll very likely end up increasing both your happiness *and* your long-term contributions at your company. This will benefit everyone.

Q: I work in a company that has a really toxic culture. I'm not sure how to improve my happiness in such a negative place. Any suggestions on dealing with a culture like that?

A: You might find it helpful to look at your work culture as a fluid thing. Work cultures aren't fixed and monolithic. Instead, they are like oceans with currents. Cultures are influenced by each employee's attitude, work style, and communication pattern.

Because of that, you may find that it's possible to establish a "micro-culture" in your section of the company.

I'm sure you've seen this before. Leliana in accounting is so kind and friendly that her positivity rubs off on those around her. There's a little warm culture bubble in her part of the company. Isabela in IT is so hostile that her group is continually impacted. She is contributing to a less friendly bubble.

You may be able to create a micro-culture that surrounds you and your work. By establishing new psychological and behavioral patterns, you may be able to generate a new set of trends—a new culture bubble around you.

Does this take effort? It certainly does. It takes determination to establish a new pattern. It also takes persistence to maintain it within a larger context that may not be aligned.

However, if you're able to do that, you'll be adding a new current to the company culture. Your wiser, warmer, kinder consciousness will be a contrast to other people's states of mind.

It's very likely that other people (particularly those who are sensitive and empathetic) will begin to align with your attractive attitudes, and help you to grow the culture bubble that you have established. Perhaps leaders in the company will even begin to follow your example.

That is how many company cultures change: not by a CEO issuing a directive, but by individual people establishing currents of kindness, warmth, and support. I encourage you to try to create your own little culture bubble, and see if it spreads.

Q: I feel guilty when I say no to anything, so I end up doing whatever my boss asks—even if I'm already overwhelmed with work. How do you deal with the fear of letting people down?

A: Let me return to one of the basic principles of cognitive therapy. Our feelings are heavily influenced by our *thoughts*. Thankfully, we can change our thought patterns so that new feelings can emerge.

If you were my client, I would begin by exploring the underlying thoughts that contribute to your feelings of worry and guilt about letting people down.

Let's imagine, for example, that you ask for help with a work project, rather than simply agreeing to add it to your plate. What thoughts pop up in that scenario?

You might find thoughts like:

"If I ask for help, my boss will lose respect for me. Maybe I'll get fired."

"Things will fall apart if I don't do this myself. Then that will be my fault."

"I should be able to handle whatever I'm asked to do. After all, that's my job."

Thoughts like those will contribute to feelings of worry, guilt, and self-pressure.

In cognitive behavioral therapy, we first identify the old, habitual thoughts as we did above. Then we begin to swap in de-pressuring, self-accepting new thoughts. Thoughts like:

"I have no idea if my boss will lose respect for me if I ask for help. Perhaps she'll actually respect my honesty! And she'd probably prefer that I don't burn out and quit."

"The world isn't on my shoulders. If things start to fall apart because I've hit a limit—well, perhaps we need to hire an additional employee or two. If we encounter challenges, we can try to address them as a team."

"I can only handle so much. My capacity isn't limitless. It's OK to let my supervisor know when I'm hitting my limit."

It will take practice for new thoughts like those to become established. This isn't simply some brief positive thinking. This is a process of retraining the mind to follow a new self-supportive path. You may need to turn your mind down the new road over and over until a new habit is formed.

To strengthen the new habit, I might encourage you to add a behavioral component to the thought repatterning.

For example, I might say, "Can we try an experiment? Tomorrow when your boss asks you to take on some additional work, can you let her know that you're happy to do so—but that your 'plate is starting to get full' and that you may need help?"

If you're willing to try a behavioral experiment like that, you might find that your old thoughts are immediately triggered. The guilty, worried thoughts and feelings might hit you like a wave. If so, you can practice allowing them to pass through as you remind yourself of your new self-accepting thoughts.

This is a core approach in cognitive behavioral therapy. We identify our old habitual thoughts, and come up with some self-supportive replacements. We then take small action steps to change our patterns. These steps usually trigger the old thoughts, which we practice replacing.

That is the general approach that I practice with my clients. It requires daily effort, but I find that it often produces very positive changes.

Q: All this psychological stuff is fine, but what I really need is more money. Do you have any ideas on how to get a raise?

A: Let me return to the win-win proposal technique to answer this one.

When my counseling clients want to ask for a raise or promotion, I usually encourage them to present their request along with an *offer* that will benefit the company (and also feel enjoyable to them). By presenting win-win proposals, they increase their chances of success.

For example, these are the type of "pitches" that I rehearse with my clients:

"I've enjoyed being a team lead over the past six months. I'm ready for additional challenges, and I'd like to request a bump up to team manager. I'd be happy to take on some HR functions in that role, and can also manage payroll. Is that something we can discuss?"

"You probably saw that my territory is doing great this past quarter. I'd like to take on a couple of adjacent territories as well. If we do that, I'd be happy to shift some of my salary over to a commission or bonus structure. I'm confident that I can raise sales for the company and also exceed my numbers. How would that feel to you?"

"I think that things have been going really well at the shop. I'd like to ask if we can bump up my hourly pay by a couple dollars. In return, I'd be happy to help out with the website and manage any upcoming events. I'm confident that we can increase sales and save money at the same time. What are your thoughts about that?"

In these examples, the people are not simply asking for a promotion or raise—they're also proposing new responsibilities that *are enjoyable to them* while benefiting the company.

It's pretty tough for managers to completely ignore friendly, win-win proposals like this. Even if the requested promotion or raise isn't possible, a manager might counter-propose something else. At the least, the process of cooperative solution-finding has been started. There may need to be some creative brainstorming, but the tone is a positive and constructive one.

Compare that to the typical way that many people ask for raises or promotions. Many employees wait patiently for a pay increase, and become increasingly upset that they are not being rewarded. They wait to say anything until they can't take it anymore. Finally, in frustration, they demand a raise.

If the company agrees, they stay. If the company declines their request, they usually start looking for a new job.

There is often a great deal of tension and hurt feelings mixed in with this process. Proactively proposing win-win solutions is much easier on both parties.

Q: I get what you're saying about the "locus of control" being out of whack. But how do you actually make changes to your locus of control?

A: The locus of control is simply a set of beliefs about your relationship to the world. As such, it can be altered with a change of thought.

One signal that your locus of control might be too large is the presence of numerous "should" and "have to" thoughts. If you find that you have thought patterns like the following:

"I *have to* get these projects done on time."
"I *should* be able to get this customer to increase his orders."
"I *shouldn't* have let that client get upset."
"I *have to* make sure my customers renew."

...then you might want to adjust those thoughts.

I have spent countless hours with my high-achieving clients finding "should," "must," and "have to" beliefs, and replacing them with statements that are less stress-producing.

For example, we can substitute these slight modifications for the thoughts above:

"I'd *very much like* to get these projects done on time."
"It *would be great* if this customer increases his orders."
"My *goal* is for my clients to be happy."
"I'm going to *do what I can* to encourage my customers to renew."

Those might seem like minor semantic changes, but they can produce an entirely different emotional experience.

If we believe that we *should, must,* and *have to* control things that are largely beyond our control, we will generate an enormous amount of stress and pressure. This is what happens when a locus of control is too large.

If we instead state that we would *like to, love to,* and are *aiming for* certain results, we're releasing the mind from self-pressuring, overly-controlling perspectives. By making changes to our thought patterns, we adjust the locus of control down in a healthy way.

What if, on the other hand, your locus of control needs to be expanded? If you find that you have thoughts like:

"It's pointless to try to accomplish this."
"The system is stacked against me."
"People never change. Why even bother to try."
"Even if I give it my best, this will end up in failure."

...then you may want to substitute more self-empowering thoughts. By doing that, you expand your locus of control and your perception of what you can impact.

The new thoughts can be realistic and humble. They don't need to be "pie in the sky" positive thinking.

For example:

"I don't know if it's pointless to try. Let me experiment with a small step or two."
"Even if the system is stacked, I can try to find little openings to make a difference."
"Some people are open to change. I can try to make an impact where I can."
"I don't know if this will end up in failure. Let's see what happens."

Those replacement thoughts aren't inflated "I can accomplish anything!" affirmations.

Instead, they are humble, realistic reminders that you can attempt changes with an open mind, and see what happens. These are locus-expanding thoughts that will help to promote a greater sense of agency and empowerment.

Your locus may need to be adjusted downward in some areas, and outward in other areas. When you feel pressured, you can look for "should" and "have to" statements, and replace those with thoughts that say, "I'd like to..." and "My aim is..."

In areas where you feel disempowered and hopeless, you can look for self-defeating and future-predicting thoughts. You can swap in new thoughts that say, "I can try to make a few changes with an open mind, and see what happens."

As you introduce both de-pressuring and empowering new beliefs, your locus of control (and the resulting emotions) will adjust.

Q: When I take breaks at work like you described, I tend to lose my focus. It breaks me out of being in the flow. Are you sure that's a good idea?

A: Being in a peaceful flow with your work is a wonderful thing. If you're in that state, by all means, please continue!

However, many people fall into a frenzied "tunnel vision" type of flow at work—and this pattern isn't healthy.

As I stated earlier, our stress circuits are essentially the same as our threat circuits. When you're in a state of stress, you're also in a state of threat. In this mode, even a thirty second break will feel like a danger. It's important not to feed this pattern.

If you are in a genuinely peaceful flow with your work, you will likely find it easy to pause for a few seconds and rest. The peaceful mind will not resist a pause.

If instead you are in a frenzied, threat-based flow, your mind will be highly resistant to pausing. It might say things like:

"I can't stop now! If I stop, I'll lose my place!"
"I don't have time to stop!"
"This has to get done—I have to push through!"
"I can rest when I'm finished. For now, I have to keep going!"

Those are the thoughts that will drive you to exhaustion. Many people spend their entire work days engaged in that type of thinking.

By pausing for a few seconds every hour, you are effectively saying, "No—I am not going to feed this type of thinking anymore. A pause is not a danger. I can take a brief pause and let the stress circuits reset. I am not going to feed these threat-based thoughts anymore."

Thirty seconds is often enough to bridge out of that stress and threat state. Even though the mind might resist the pauses at first, those breaks will restore peace and very likely increase your productivity in the long run.

Through practice, the mind will learn how valuable they are.

Q: *I really have no idea how to choose a higher purpose for my work. My job is just a job. Are you supposed to just make something up?*

A: Let me return to an idea I presented earlier in this book. We bring meaning to our work. Our work does not bring meaning to us.

We decide what gifts and talents to offer through our work. We also decide *why* we are giving those gifts and talents. This is why setting a purpose is so important. A chosen purpose not only directs your activities, but also shapes your emotional experience of your work.

I have counseled clients who went into health care, public service, education, and non-profit sectors because they wanted to do something meaningful. But what many of them found was "just another job."

When I work with these clients, I encourage them to select a purpose for their work that aligns with their own values—and then channel their work activities toward serving that purpose. It is that purposeful direction that creates a sense of meaning.

Even if you feel that your job is "just a job," you can choose a purpose for it that brings you fulfillment.

For example, here are some purpose statements that I have heard from people:

> My purpose at work is to grow by developing my skills and knowledge.
> My purpose at work is to create a positive experience for my direct reports.
> My purpose at work is to practice being patient with people.

You can choose any purpose for your work that brings you a sense of fulfillment and satisfaction. That chosen purpose will be a lamp that lights your path.

As you set a purpose, and keep it in mind throughout your day, you may find that your experience of your job begins to shift. Or you may instead realize that you can serve your purpose more fully in a different job or career path, and begin to make a change.

Setting a purpose for your work can create a shift in perspective that clarifies your career landscape and guides your steps. I encourage you to choose something personally meaningful, and begin to direct your activities toward that destination.

•

Let me conclude this chapter by giving a summary of the five techniques I covered. All five of these approaches can be used together.

To begin your day, you can prioritize the goal of *doing your work in an enjoyable way*. You may need to remind yourself of this goal throughout the day, especially when you feel yourself falling into unhealthy levels of stress. You get to define what enjoyable work means to you.

In order to serve this goal, you can seek win-win solutions throughout your work day. This involves proposing solutions that benefit you and your company, and also inviting ideas for such solutions from others. As you practice finding mutually beneficial arrangements, it's very likely that your work fulfillment will increase.

It may be important to adjust your locus of control so that you don't feel pressured and responsible for outcomes that are beyond your control. Many companies will encourage an overly large locus of control by saying things like, "You can do anything if you try hard enough!" It's important not to let these apparently empowering statements lead to over-pressuring dynamics.

Throughout the day, you can take breaks, preferably every hour. These break times, which might be as little as a few seconds, are designed to let the stress circuits release and reset. If you find it helpful, you can use the "waves" technique to allow your feelings and thoughts to pass through you like a wave.

As you center yourself in the present moment, and give your feelings and thoughts permission to pass through you, you may be able to touch into a place of greater calm and peace. Even a few seconds spent in this place can be restorative.

Perhaps above all else, it can be helpful to set a purpose for your work. No matter what you do in your job, you can dedicate your work to serving a mission that aligns with your values. As you choose a purpose, and channel your efforts to align with that purpose, you may find that your sense of meaning and fulfillment increases.

Let me now conclude this book with an "action steps" section that contains behavioral stretches, worksheets, lists of careers, business ideas, and other information to support the various chapters in this book.

CHAPTER FOURTEEN

Action Steps

In this chapter, I will share a variety of tools that can help to convert the ideas in this book into action.

To begin, let me share some "stretch steps" for each facet of the career development process. As a behavioral therapist, I encourage my counseling clients to stretch their behaviors in gentle ways each day. A series of small stretches can lead surprisingly quickly to new experiences.

Along those lines, I encourage you to read through the following action steps and note which ones trigger a sense of *resistance* in your mind. Those might turn out to be the most powerful ones to work on in the end.

Also notice which of these steps feel *easiest* to practice. Those might be the best ones to start with. We always want to get a momentum going. Beginning with the easiest steps while working toward more resistant areas is usually a good strategy.

Exploring Career Paths

Stretch to consider career paths that might be outside your immediate area of expertise.

Career exploration involves opening the mind. In order to feel the "pull"—the inner sense of what draws your interest—it can be helpful to clear the mind of limiting preconceived notions.

When considering a career path, your mind might tell you that you're too young, too old, too technical, too creative, too introverted, too extroverted, or something else. Try to release those thoughts. Consider career paths as broadly as possible, without self-limiting beliefs. Stretch to open your mind as wide as possible as you're considering various career options.

Stretch to chat with people about their work experience.

There is no substitute for direct conversations with people about their work. Would you like to know what it's like to be a barista in a coffee shop? Many baristas would be happy to share their experience with you. How about a postal worker, or a firefighter, or a marriage license clerk? People who are working in those roles can give you an inside look at their work lives.

You may be thinking, "I don't want to bother anyone." But many people will be honored that you're interested in their work experience. Some may even be excited to "recruit" you into their field. Try to stretch by initiating conversations with people in fields that you find interesting. You can do this in person, by email, or by sending folks a LinkedIn or Facebook message.

Job Searching

Stretch to look for job postings that are in unusual places.

Most of my career counseling clients settle into a habit of checking a handful of job posting websites over and over. I always encourage them to stretch by finding, bookmarking, and regularly checking sites outside their typical pattern.

There are hundreds of niche job posting sites in specialty fields and regions. There are also many government job posting sites on the city, county, state, and federal level. Generally, none of these sites will have any overlap with the others. Stretch to find and check these specialty sites. You may be one of only a few candidates who see the jobs posted there.

Stretch to consider posting your resume, if it's safe for you to do so.

Let me once again underscore that it can be a risk to post your resume. Your employer (or a recruiter who works with your employer) may see your resume and assume that you're preparing to quit your job. Please *only* post your resume if you are truly comfortable doing so, and confident that it will not put you at risk.

If that is the case, doing so can be very productive. You can use a dedicated Gmail and Google Voice number on your resume to screen contacts accordingly. You can include a comment about your target relocation areas, job type, or other parameters. You can also tag "open to work" on your LinkedIn profile. If it's safe for you to do so, this can be a great stretch step to find new opportunities.

Stretch to have conversations with people about the gifts and skills you are excited to offer.

As I mentioned earlier, up to 80% of jobs are found through conversations and interpersonal connections. It may feel a bit vulnerable or exposing to let people know that you're interested in new opportunities. However, that type of stretch can produce significant results.

If the traditional "networking" approach doesn't appeal to you, you can flip the script and simply focus on giving. You can let people know how eager you are to help, and share ideas about how you would like to use your gifts. In this way, networking becomes an offer of help rather than a request for job leads. That shift can change the emotional impact of the experience.

Applying for Jobs

Stretch to apply for jobs that are "in the ballpark," even if you're not sure that they're a fit.

I spend a great deal of time encouraging my counseling clients to consider job opportunities that seem like imperfect fits. I tell them, "We really don't know what this job will be like. You might have a great connection with the people there, or you might not. The job responsibilities might be flexible, or they might not. There's no way to tell that from a job ad."

I then encourage them to apply for openings that are "in the ballpark" as an exploration process. I encourage you to stretch your scope as well. Once you actually talk to a recruiter or hiring manager at a company, you can describe your goals, skills, values, and interests. At that point, it will become clearer if there is a good match from both sides. If you stretch to apply for "imperfect" jobs, it can help to start these conversations.

Stretch to tailor your resume and cover letter to match the position.

I have read stories of people who applied for over 1000 jobs without receiving any response. If those stories are accurate, I imagine that the applicant is blasting out a non-customized resume without a cover letter. A far better approach is to slightly customize your resume and cover letter to highlight the matches between your background and the job at hand.

I encourage you to stretch by spending at least five minutes to edit the summary section on your resume, re-order your bullets, and customize a brief cover letter to show the matches. When you do this, you make it almost impossible for recruiters to put you in a "not a fit" category. A stretch to customize can help enormously to open doors.

ACTION STEPS

Interviewing

Stretch to find connections with your interviewer.

Everyone wants to feel that they are in the company of a friend. You can help to create this sense of kinship by finding connections with your interviewer, and referencing those in your conversations.

Perhaps your interviewer used to live in the same part of the country that you did. Perhaps you both have an interest in a sport. Perhaps you and she are both connected to a common person on LinkedIn. By doing a little research, you may be able to find those connections. If there are no apparent commonalities up front, you can look for them throughout your conversation. Stretch to seek those connections, point them out, and foster a sense of kinship.

Stretch to highlight how you can help.

It's very likely that your mind will tell you that you need to impress people during the interview process—that you need to get their approval and get the job. I encourage you to stretch by moving in the opposite direction. Instead of trying to *get* approval, you can focus instead on all that you have to *give*.

Express your enthusiasm to give and help. Share stories about how you have given and helped in past jobs. Mention ways that you are excited to support the organization and its people. As you do that, it's very likely that your interviewer will "reflexively empathize" with your enthusiastic, giving-oriented mindset, and feel delighted about the potential to work together. By focusing on giving, rather than getting, you will very likely make the best impression possible.

Stretch to learn details about the company

A large number of the people I interview as a recruiter know very little about the company they are applying to work with. Some candidates haven't even taken time to read through the company's website when they interview with me.

If you stretch to learn about the company you're interviewing with, it can only help. Read through their website, including any news items or press releases. Look them up on LinkedIn and see how many employees they have. Learn about their history. And then reference this information in the interview. You will stand out far more than other candidates who didn't take the time to do that.

Self-Employment

Stretch to learn about the needs of people and companies.

Many entrepreneurs start a business by offering services or products that they are personally excited about. If it turns out that there is a need for that offering, the business booms. If not, the business struggles to build a customer base.

Instead of taking an "if you build it, they will come" approach, I encourage you to stretch by *first* learning about what the people and organizations around you need. *Then* ask yourself what exciting products and services can fill those needs. It takes a bit of work up front to learn about people's needs and desires. But the more you understand the mindset of your potential customers, the more likely you'll be to offer something truly helpful.

Stretch to broaden your business mix at the beginning.

Recall the three-dimensional cube model. Most people settle on a single point in the cube. However, especially at the beginning stages of a business, it may be helpful to expand the scope of your offerings.

If you're planning to offer a service, consider adding a product as well. If you're considering a tangible product, consider a digital or ideas-oriented one as a compliment. If you're planning to run your business by yourself, consider including a consultant or contractor in the mix to help you out. Stretch to expand your conception of your business structure and offerings. Once you find your niche, you can narrow to what works. But at the outset, it can be helpful to cast a wide net.

Stretch to find referral sources.

It's essential to get the word out about the products and services you're offering. You can do that by outreach to potential customers. However, you can also reach out to people who *interact* with your potential customers. Stretch to identify, locate, and build relationships with these people.

In my psychotherapy practice, I've received referrals from nurse practitioners, therapists, professors, and parole officers. These people all interacted with large numbers of people who were seeking counseling. I've also served as a referral source for many of these people myself. Think about who might interact with potential customers of yours, and stretch to develop those relationships.

Improving your Work Life

Stretch to use the five techniques I outlined.

Many people read through tools like the ones I outlined, but don't actually apply them on a day-to-day basis. I encourage you to stretch to make these daily habits. To briefly summarize the five approaches one last time:

Set a top goal of doing your work in a way that is enjoyable and emotionally healthy. Move any other goals after this one.

Seek for, propose, and solicit win-win solutions throughout your work day. A win-win solution is one that both you and other people feel good about.

Recognize what is within your power, and what isn't, and adjust your "locus of control" accordingly. Do not take over responsibility for things that are outside your control. Do proactively apply your creative efforts and skills to improve what is within your control.

Stop for a few seconds every hour to let your stress circuits relax. Set an hourly alarm on your phone or computer if you find it helpful. During these times, let your mind relax. Don't give in to the belief that you have to endlessly "push through" things without a break.

Set a higher purpose for your work, in addition to making money. You get to choose this, and your choice of purpose will shape your entire experience of your work. It will give meaning to what you do. A shift in purpose can alter the entire landscape of your career.

Worksheets

Let me now offer copies of some worksheets that can help you apply the ideas in this book. I encourage you to actually fill out these worksheets, as a way of clarifying your thoughts.

You can download PDF versions of these worksheets for printing by visiting my www.ColoradoCounseling.com site and going to the worksheets section.

ACTION STEPS

Worksheet
Career Exploration: The Five Questions

These five questions can help to clarify some areas to explore further. It may be helpful to clear the mind of any preconceived notions or ideas as you consider these.

Career Exploration: The Five Questions

1. How excited are you to set up your own business?

Not in the slightest!	Possibly. I'm on the fence.	I can't imagine doing anything else!

Working for an established company may be best. Let's move to the next question.

Let's check: Will you be comfortable being in "sales mode"? Will you be able to handle many different roles? Will you be able to set your own schedule each day? Can you handle ebb-and-flow income? If so, self-employment may be a great fit.

2. Are you interested in for-profit, non-profit, or "middle-way" organizations like educational, government, and health care companies?

For-profit (banks, manufacturing, coffee shops)	Middle-way (universities, hospitals, fire departments)	Non-profit (animal shelters, social service agencies, group homes)

3. How big of a company might you like to work for?

5 people or less	500 people	5000 people or more

4. What type of work environment appeals to you? And how much social interaction would you like? Here are a few examples:

Outdoor environments	Airports	Very little social interaction
Retail stores	In a vehicle	Interaction only when I want
Offices at a desk	Ships	Balance of social/alone time
Academic campuses	Home office	A good deal of interaction
Warehouses	Hospitals	Never alone at work

5. How much of your time and energy would you like to give to work?

The minimum possible!	I want a reasonable work/life balance.	I want work that fuses with the rest of my life.

Worksheet
Daily Practice Record

You can use this practice record to keep track of progress on any new behavioral habit, including your job search. Remember that 5 to 15 minutes a day will likely produce excellent forward momentum.

Daily Practice Record

My goal for the week:

I am willing to spend _____ minutes/day taking steps toward this goal.

List of Possible Steps: 1.   4.
                                          2.   5.
                                          3.   6.

Monday	Tuesday	Wednesday	Thursday	Friday
Steps taken:	Steps taken:	Steps taken:	Steps taken:	Steps taken:
Experience/ result:	Experience/ result:	Experience/ result:	Experience/ result:	Experience/ result:

ACTION STEPS

Template
Simple Resume

You can keep your resume simple. Feel free to model it after this basic format. Remember that the *matches* between your background and the job you're applying for are important to highlight. Your summary and first few bullets should show those.

Your Name
City, State
email@fairexec.com
(303) 555-1000

SUMMARY

Include a two sentence summary that describes your background and skills. Please customize this *slightly* for each job you apply for.

EXPERIENCE

First Company
Title
2020-present

You can include a one-sentence description of the company here, if the company isn't well known.

- Include four to seven bullets for each job.
- The best format is to start with a *verb*, followed by a *description* of your responsibilities and (if possible) a *result*.
- Please re-order and slightly customize the first couple bullets to match with the job you're applying for. Those are the most important.

Second Company
Title
2015-present

- Same for each of your past jobs.

EDUCATION

You can list degrees, coursework, and certifications/trainings here.

SKILLS

If you wish, you can add a "skills" section. You can also add "interests" or "volunteer experience" if you have room that you need to fill up.

Template
Simple Cover Letter

I recommend a simple, three-paragraph cover letter. The first paragraph introduces you and states the position you're applying for. The second paragraph points out a few matches between your background and the job. The third paragraph is a wrap-up.

> Dear Hiring Manager:
>
> I am interested in applying for your [name of the job] position. My experience as a [briefly describe the connection between your background and the job.]
>
> In my previous position at [name a past job], I [point out a few elements from your resume that are the strongest matches between your background and the job you're applying for.] At [name a second past job], I [point out another match between a past job and this one you're applying for.]
>
> I am available to speak to you by phone or through a video conference. My cell phone is (303) 555-1000 and my email is email@fairexec.com. Thank you for your consideration.
>
> Sincerely,
> Your Name

Certainly feel free to modify this as you wish, but try to keep things as concise as you can. Remember that you may have less than thirty seconds (and perhaps as few as six seconds) to hold your reader's attention.

ACTION STEPS

Worksheet
Interview Questions

It's best to prepare answers to these questions for each company you interview with. Questions 2 through 4 may stay the same, but Question 1 should be customized for each position. Remember that stories are powerful ways to communicate.

The Four Interview Questions

1. What interests you about *this particular job* that you're interviewing for? (You can mention the job responsibilities, specifics about the company, shared values, etc.)

2. Why are you interested in a new position at this time? (You can be as honest as you'd like. For a general answer, you can talk about how you're "interested in new challenges." But then do give more detail.)

3. Can you give a story or two of a "success" at work?

4. Can you give a story or two of a work "challenge you learned from"?

Career Lists

Let me share a series of career and job lists organized by topic. These lists are not exhaustive. They are simply designed to spark your creative circuits and lead to further exploration.

I also encourage you to explore the O*NET OnLine site at www.onetonline.org which contains customized lists based on your O*NET Interest Profiler results. There are thousands of jobs on the O*NET site, organized by categories.

As you read through these lists, try to get a sense of where your "inner compass" might be pulling you. Note when you feel an emotional spark. When that happens, you might want to explore that type of job—and related ones—more fully.

Careers for people who like to be outdoors

Landscaper	Parks and rec worker
Farmer	Roofer
Forest service worker	Exterior painter
Road maintenance worker	Stone mason
Surveyor	Wilderness guide
Ski instructor	Arborist
Environmental technician	Oil and gas field worker
Electrical utility worker	Logger
Solar panel installer	Dog walker
Geologist	Wildlife control officer

Careers in skilled trades
(many of which have apprenticeship programs)

Carpenter	Electrician
Plumber	Pipe/steam fitter
Stone/brick mason	Cement/concrete mason

ACTION STEPS

HVAC
Boilermaker
Glazier/glass worker
Sheet metal worker
Fire sprinkler fitter
Flooring specialist
Welder
Ironworker
Drywall installer
Tile setter
Roofer
Fence construction
Solar energy installer
Mechanic

Careers for people who like numbers

Engineer
Statistician
Accountant
Physical scientist
Supply chain analyst
Banker
Cryptographer
Insurance adjuster
HR compensation analyst
Auditor
Financial analyst
Math teacher/professor
Actuary
Data scientist
Computer systems modeler
Systems analyst
Database administrator
Loan officer
Financial securities trader
Estimator

Careers for people who like words

Advertising copywriter
Copy editor
Executive editor
Journalist
Technical writer
Counselor
Marketing communications
Public policy professional
eLearning content creator
Public relations specialist
Translator
Teacher
Sales professional
Librarian
Social media manager
Corporate trainer
Transcriber
Attorney
Paralegal
Religious professional

Careers for people who are visually-oriented

Photo editor	Architect
Painter	Interior designer
Fashion designer	Marketing communications
Advertising executive	Product designer
Brand manager	Videographer/video editor
Art director	Graphic designer
Layout designer	Photographers
Illustrators	User experience designer
Art teacher	Video game designer
Filmmaker	Fine artist

Careers for people who like movement

Postal mail carriers	Retail store workers
Personal trainer	Yoga instructor
Building inspector	Property manager
Massage therapist	Mechanic
Pre-school teacher	Restaurant server
Construction worker	Groundskeeper
Plumber	Carpenter
Police officer	Firefighter
Physical therapist	Many military roles
Housekeeper	Repair professionals

Careers that focus on helping vulnerable people

Nurse	Firefighter
Teacher	Psychologist
School counselor	Physician/physician assistant
Case manager	Medical assistant
Marriage and family therapist	Mental health counselor

ACTION STEPS

Non-profit professional
District attorney
Addictions counselor
Child protective
services worker
Paramedic

Public defender
Police officers
Social worker
Physical or
occupational therapist
Nursing home staff

Careers for people who like to be around food

Chef/cook
Caterer
Restaurant server
Line/prep cook
Food delivery driver
Agricultural worker
Food inspector
Specialty foods marketer
Restaurant busser
Pastry chef

Food production worker
Bartender
Cafeteria worker
Restaurant host/hostess
Restaurant manager
Grocery store staff
Barista
Food distribution worker
Food scientist
Dietitian

Careers that can be done remotely or virtually

Virtual admin assistant
Writer
Customer service rep
IT professional
Proofreader
Software programmer
Internet-based researcher
Life coach
Customer service rep
Appointment setter (sales)

Website creator
Graphic designer
Account manager
Editor
Medical transcriber
Online tutor/teacher
Software tester/QA
Data scientist/analyst
Technical support
Marketing consultant

Careers that involve travel or transportation

Delivery driver	Travel agent
Cargo ship crew	Flight attendant
Long-haul truck driver	Pilot
Rail yard worker	Tourism sales rep
Rideshare driver	Highway maintenance worker
Cruise ship staff	Dock worker
Tour guide	Bus driver
Distribution analyst	Airline ticketing agent
Rental car agency staff	Air traffic controller
Train engineer	Airport concessions worker

Careers for people who are introverted

Forestry worker	Technical writer
Laboratory technician	Video editor
Software Test/QA	Visual artist
Business analyst	Engineer
Graphic designer	Assembler/production worker
Mechanic	Accountant
Website coder	Truck driver
Repair technician	Researcher
Farmer	Medical coder
Tree/lawn care worker	Database analyst

Careers for people who are extroverted

Sales/account rep	Nurse
Corporate trainer	HR generalist
Attorney	Marketing specialist
Event planner	Teacher
Recruiter	Office manager

ACTION STEPS

Customer service rep Social media manager
Physical therapist Team manager
Realtor Social worker
Store manager Bank teller
Restaurant server Reporter

Let me share a caveat on these lists: I can think of numerous people in these careers who don't "fit" the heading. For example, I myself am very introverted by nature—but I work in typically "extroverted careers" as a recruiter and counselor.

You can explore any career that you'd like, no matter how it's classified or described. Your inner compass—your inner sense of what interests you—will guide you in its own unique way.

Finally, let me share a list of thirty small business ideas that don't require special degrees or a great deal of investment capital.

If you want to pursue the path of self-employment, see if any of these draw you. (But remember that it's always best to start by investigating the needs of people and companies around you.)

Small Businesses to Consider

House painting Business lead generation
Personal training Written content creation
Academic tutoring Website design
Marketing consulting Handyperson/home repair
Landscaping/lawn care Professional organizing
Moving/transportation Videography
Sewing/alterations Interior decorating
Home inspection Graphic design
Pet walking/sitting Internet-based reseller
Life coaching Car detailing
House cleaning Internet marketing/SEO
Personal/virtual assistance Event planning

Computer/IT consulting
Athletics coach/instructor
Child care

Catering
Property management
Bookkeeping

•

Links for Job Openings

Although there are new job posting websites that pop up frequently, the following are some that you may want to explore.

The Big Five:

Indeed: www.indeed.com
LinkedIn: www.linkedin.com/jobs
Monster: www.monster.com
Glassdoor: www.glassdoor.com
ZipRecruiter: www.ziprecruiter.com

Another Five:

Craigslist (small companies): www.craigslist.org
SimplyHired (aggregator): www.simplyhired.com
CareerBuilder: www.careerbuilder.com
Dice (technical jobs): www.dice.com
Upwork (freelance jobs): www.upwork.com

Specialty Sites:

There are hundreds of specialty job posting sites, including those for veterans, skilled trades, nursing, philanthropy, higher education, countless technical disciplines, and more. If you belong to a professional association or society, trade union, or other industry group, that type of organization can be a great place to start looking for these specialty sites. Otherwise, a simple internet search for "[your field] job site" may point you to some.

Workforce Centers:

Each state offers a "job bank" of local job listings at state-run workforce centers. (Your state may use a different term like "job center" or "career center.")

In addition to job listings, workforce centers often offer free career counseling, resume writing assistance, and other forms of career support. Please consider using these services. Your taxes have already paid for them!

To find your local workforce center, try searching on "[your county] workforce center" or visit your state's Department of Labor website.

Alternatively, you can go to www.careeronestop.org and click on the "find local help" menu to search by zip code. Note that this site calls workforce centers "American Job Centers."

Federal Government jobs:

Most federal-level government positions are located at the website www.USAJobs.gov. However, there are some federal agencies that aren't required to use the site—so you may also want to visit the careers page at any specific agency you're interested in (CDC, EPA, USPS, etc.)

State Government jobs:

Each state has its own site for jobs with the state government. Please note that these sites are *not* the same as the workforce centers, listed above. To find state government jobs, you can search on "[your state] government jobs."

County and City Government jobs:

You'll need to search on individual cities and counties for a list of jobs at the local government level. Note that there are unusual government structures in some states. For example, Alaska, Connecticut, and Rhode Island don't have county governments. You'll have to check at the city or state level there.

As I mentioned, the more "hidden" your local city and county government job sites are, the less competition you'll have. You can search on "government jobs in [city/county of _____]."

Companies:

Individual company websites may list hundreds (or even thousands) of job openings. Many of these won't be posted elsewhere. Please make sure to visit any companies and organizations that you like. These can include for-profit companies, non-profits, and middle-way organizations like universities, schools, and hospitals.

•

Final Note

As a final note, I want to acknowledge that it can be challenging to develop a fulfilling career. Many of us struggle to attend to the demands of our day-to-day lives. The idea of looking for a new career or job on top of that seems daunting.

And yet—I have known many people who were able to move from unfulfilling, emotionally draining work situations into new employment that felt remarkably right. I have known other people who were able to make positive changes at their current jobs, and found a greater sense of happiness (and often a raise). Improvements can happen.

ACTION STEPS

I am a great believer that your "inner compass"—your inner sense of what is right for you—will guide you along your career path. Your inner wisdom will prompt you when it's time to make a change, and it will nudge you toward new areas to explore. Keeping an open mind helps this wisdom to arise.

Finally, you don't need to take your career journey alone. Even if you can't afford sessions with a professional career counselor, there are many affordable resources to draw upon.

Your state-run "workforce centers" (also known as "American Job Centers") will likely offer free career support services, including resume writing and job search assistance. Your high school or college may also offer career services, even if you've already graduated.

In addition, most counseling and psychology graduate schools offer low-cost counseling to the community so that their graduate students can gain experience. Even new counselors and therapists who don't specialize in career issues will be happy to discuss your work life with you. They may be surprisingly helpful.

If you have questions about anything you have read in this book, you are welcome to email me. I will need to be brief in my replies, but I'm happy to clarify anything that is unclear. The best way to reach me is through my website at www.DanJoseph.com.

I wish you the best in your career journey.

About the Author

Dan Joseph Cavicchio is a Licensed Professional Counselor and National Certified Counselor specializing in career counseling and cognitive behavioral therapy. Dan founded Colorado Counseling, LLC as a sliding-scale therapy practice in 2009.

Dan is also an executive and technical recruiter. He is the president of Fairfield Technology Search, LLC and Fairfield Executive Search, LLC. Although he has completed searches for Fortune 500 clients, he specializes in work with small to mid-sized companies, including startups.

Dan invites you to follow or connect with him on Linkedin at www.linkedin.com/in/cavicchio. He can also be contacted via his author website at www.DanJoseph.com.

www.ingramcontent.com/pod-product-compliance
Lightning Source LLC
Chambersburg PA
CBHW020630220526
45464CB00001B/93